HOW TO

BEAT POLICE RADAR . . .

and Do It Legally

HOW TO BEAT POLICE RADAR . . . and Do It Legally

Rex Power

ARCO PUBLISHING COMPANY, INC.
NEW YORK

Published by Arco Publishing Company, Inc.
219 Park Avenue South, New York, N.Y. 10003

Portions of this book were originally published in a pamphlet entitled *How to Beat Police Radar,* copyright © 1976 by Consolidated Western Industries, Publications Division, Washington, D.C.

Library of Congress Cataloging in Publication Data

Power, Rex
How to beat police radar . . . and do it legally.

Includes index.
1. Radar in speed limit enforcement—United States.
I. Title.

HV8079.5.P68 363.2'33 77-6688
ISBN 0-668-04317-2 (Library Edition)
ISBN 0-668-04322-9 (Paper Edition)

Printed in the United States of America

With great appreciation to

R.C.L. *and* R.L.

without whose efforts this book would not have been possible.

WARNING

Nothing in this book should be taken as an invitation to break any law. This book is designed to supply the latest information to motorists, police forces, and judges concerning the strong points and weaknesses of radar as an effective motor vehicle speed control device. I sincerely believe that laws should not just be obeyed but vigorously enforced. Reckless speeders are a menace to society and should be removed from our roads and highways. However, many careful drivers receive speeding tickets, and are convicted for offenses which they never committed. It is in the interest of justice and highway safety that this book is written.

REX POWER

ENTRAPMENT

The act of officers or agents of the government in inducing a person to commit a crime not contemplated by him, for the purpose of instituting a criminal prosecution against him.

Contents

CHAPTER 1

The Problem

Police across the nation are conducting massive crackdowns on speeders through the use of radiopositioning equipment, better known as radar. In just one state, Maryland, police have arrested as many as 3,000 speeders per day with a variety of radar devices.

Motorists are used to periodic crackdowns by police agencies out to prove to the newspapers, politicians, or to the public that they are doing their job. But a new incentive has been added. Since the energy crisis came upon us and Congress in its wisdom passed a law establishing the national speed limit at 55-miles-per-hour, more pressure is being applied to policemen to enforce, to the limit, the law concerning speeding violations.

According to this law, which is intended to "conserve fuel and increase safety," all states must establish their maximum speed limits on every highway no higher than 55 miles-per-hour, with the exception that "emergency and public motor vehicles may be authorized to operate at higher speeds when necessary to protect health or safety."

Should the Secretary of Transportation determine that a particular state has failed to comply with this rule, that state would risk loss of its federal highway project funds. Therefore, as published in the *Federal Register* of June 9, 1975, each state must provide the Federal Highway Administration with a statement containing:

1. A copy of its speed limit law, regulation, or administrative order, including the sanctions for its violation;
2. An opinion of the state's legal counsel that the law is valid;
3. Notice that the speed limit signs have been changed where necessary.

Then, in a second *Federal Register* notice issued the same day, the Department of Transportation put more pressure on the states by insisting a procedure be adopted by which the states would have to certify their enforcement of the 55 mile-per-hour limit. The proposal, DOT said, "should serve to lighten the administrative burden of complying with the regulation," calling for an unspecified volume of data and content that is not beyond what DOT termed "the bare minimum which is generally essential to statistical credibility."

On July 30, 1975, the Insurance Institute for Highway Safety reported in its *Status Report* that FHWA had said that comments on the previous certification procedure proposal had objected to "what was seen as a federal assumption that the states could not be trusted to enforce the speed limit."

In this same *Status Report,* it was reported that the governors were up in arms over these guidelines they must follow to certify that the congressionally mandated 55 mile-per-hour speed limit was being enforced. They cried out that this would lead to "construction of a new federal speed enforcement bureaucracy" that would be "expensive, unnecessary, inappropriate, and constitutionally repugnant."

The June 9 proposal called for a certification of enforcement including:

1. A statement signed by the governor certifying the law's enforcement;
2. Copies of state laws, regulations, or administrative orders subsequent to a state's previous submission on compliance;
3. Information on enforcement, including the number of citations issued by the state for violations of the 55 mile-per-hour limit during each month of the previous year;
4. Information on motorists' observance of the speed limit laws, including a description of the monitoring program used and a summary of the data obtained from such a program.

The DOT regulation further demands that each state must submit a complete certification of enforcement by January 1 of each year.

With all this pressure being put on the states it is no wonder radar is being employed to rack up an impressive speed trap record. The best way to prove enforcement is to compile a large list of arrests, and that's exactly what is happening.

Radar is the weapon being used! According to the Federal Communications Commission, the states licensed for the greatest number of radiopositioning units are: North Carolina, Ohio, Illinois, Mississippi, Maryland, Arizona, Oklahoma, Georgia, South Carolina, Indiana, Iowa, Kansas, Missouri, and South Dakota. You are correct in assuming that the most massive radar conducted speeder hunts are in these states.

Maryland, in February, 1977, launched an operation called "Yellow Jacket"—this state's big new crackdown on speeders. The Maryland State Troopers involved in the program actually drive cruisers decorated with the operation's insignia—an irate bee aiming a radar gun at an unseen offender.

This does not mean that you are safe in other states. Far from it! Radar is being used to trap speeders in all 50 states, Guam, Puerto Rico, and throughout Canada and in areas of Mexico. The combination of powerful automobiles, good roads, and the reduced speed limits puts every driver in severe danger of being cited for speed infractions each time he drives his car.

In October, 1976, the American Automobile Association added Virginia and New Mexico to its list of states that strictly enforce the nationwide 55 mile-per-hour limit. AAA defines such strict enforcement as "one in which an abnormally high number of traffic citations is issued in a given period of time." The other states already listed on the AAA rolls are: Maryland, Massachusetts, and New Hampshire and parts of Kentucky, Louisiana, New Jersey, Ohio, Pennsylvania, Tennessee, and West Virginia.

The Long Island State Park and Recreation Commission even got into the act last summer announcing that a special police radar patrol would start operating on three major parkways in Nassau and Suffolk Counties in an effort to reduce "flagrant violations" of the speed limit. The project was financed under a $125,453 grant from the federal government and with the approval of the Governor's interdepartmental traffic safety committee. The project involved a fleet of marked radar patrol cars, seven days a week, 24 hours a day, for an indefinite period.

According to the Federal Communications Commission records on radiopositioning licenses, even police forces on college campuses are now employing these devices. In point of fact, almost every imaginable police agency of any kind has some type of radar. Why? Universities would not be affected by a cutback in federal HEW funds should they fail to control speeders on their respective campuses. The answer is really quite simple. It is a perfect way to fatten up their bank accounts without further demands on the tuition schedule. Speeding tickets are a perfect way to help balance budgets.

Needless to say, this holds true for municipalities, too. Handing out speeding tickets is a much better way of gathering revenue than by raising school taxes, sewer usage fees, or property taxes. It is a beautiful "out" for politicians.

This is a true story. One town in Alabama—Fruithurst—located on the Alabama/Georgia line is famous as a "speed trap" town. The town, with a population of 250, used speeding tickets as its major source of revenue. In one year it actually collected in excess of $200,000 in fines and forfeitures. Fruithurst was named the worst speed trap in the nation. Things became so bad that State Attorney General, William J. Baxley, volunteered to represent any citizen in a civil suit against the town.

Fruithurst was not the only town using speed traps to fatten its coffers. It was perhaps the most flagrant, but there are plenty of others taking advantage of unsuspecting motorists right now.

In states where radar crackdown is sporadic, drivers are lulled into a false sense of security. If you drive a certain roadway each day and if everyone always hits 60 miles-per-hour or better on it, you become a sitting duck for a radiopositioning unit that decides to "catch a few fish today."

Later in 1977 a State of Texas legislator, Representative Bennie Bock of New Braunfels will try to pass legislation that limits the number of fines levied for speeding citations in Texas. This will be his third attempt to reduce the incentive for the operation of speed traps in the town of Selma, a community sitting at Interstate 35 between San Antonio and New Braunfels. The law, if passed, would apply statewide.

Known in the region as the "valley of the bears," Mr. Bock has accused Selma police officers of sitting along parts of Interstate 35 after dark without parking lights in an all-out effort to nab speeders. He contends that it is, in fact, illegal to park on the highway without parking lights.

The other thing they do that is so bad, according to Mr. Bock, is to kite tickets. This means if a driver is caught doing 60 miles-per-hour, the trooper might enter 65 or 70 on the citation. If you happen to be from out of town or state, you either pay up immediately or come back later for a court hearing.

The proposal Mr. Bock has suggested would not have any effect on the practice of ticket kiting, but it would demand that a program of uniform fines be introduced throughout the State of Texas. Under his bill, motorists cited for exceeding posted limits from one to five miles over could be fined no more than $1 for each excessive mile of speed.

Some new technical devices are now being used as part of the nationwide crackdown. These include radar-equipped helicopters, hand-held, portable radar units, radar-equipped unmarked cars including VW's, Mercedes-Benz', pick-up trucks, and even garbage trucks to bolster the fleets of unmarked cars already patrolling the nation's highways, secondary roads, and streets.

In many states, police are now using small radar units that can be plugged into the car's cigarette lighter socket and are able to clock traffic in both directions.

Police are also using a new radar "Speed Gun" which looks like a small Buck Rogers pistol. It can be pointed at a car one mile away and register its speed.

A Maryland State Trooper explains the "Speed Gun's" operation: "If you want to clock the speed of a car you just aim it and squeeze the trigger. Numbers, like those on a digital watch, light up on the back of the gun and display the rate of speed. It is accurate within one mile-per-hour." This trooper nailed 60 speeders in four hours with the new "Speed Gun" one summer afternoon while sitting on a bridge spanning the Washington, D.C. beltway, Interstate 495.

As with the helicopter units, a speeder is clocked by one officer who radios to a chase car down the highway which pulls the motorist over and issues the ticket.

When you realize the cost of a speeding ticket it is easy to see why radar traps are so favorable. Across the U.S. fines for speed violations range from a set fine of $5 to a fine of $1,000. Most states have also adopted a point system. For example, the Commonwealth of Pennsylvania fines speeders a basic $35 for the infraction, $10 for the magistrate, and then $2 a mile for every mile above 5 miles over the speed limit. In addition, Pennsylvanians get points on their record. They are charged as follows:

EXCEEDING MAXIMUM SPEED LIMIT	
6 to 10 miles over	2 points
11 to 15 miles over	3 points
16 to 25 miles over	4 points

26 to 30 miles over.................................5 points
31 miles and over...................................5 points & departmental hearing and sanctions.

When a driver's record shows an aggregate of six points, he will receive notice to attend driver improvement school or undergo a special examination. If it happens twice, drivers can have their licenses suspended for up to 15 days.

The State of Maryland subjects motorists to a $30 fine; from 10 to 19 miles-per-hour over could cost $40 and from 20 to 29 miles over could cost $50. Anything over this and it could be a court appearance plus $150 if found guilty.

Motorists guilty of driving six to sixteen miles over the 55 mile-per-hour limit would be charged up to $1.75 for each mile, and those convicted of driving sixteen miles-per-hour and more could receive a fine of $2 for each mile over the legal limit.

Not all the monies collected would go to the municipalities. The bill provides that half of the money would go to the states on Interstate citations.

So when the State of Maryland issues 3,000 citations per day, statewide, at an average of $30 per ticket, that adds up to a healthy input of monies totalling $90,000.

In the first five months of 1976 the Commonwealth of Pennsylvania pulled in some $4,051,260 from speeding tickets, using $30 as the average fine. Pennsylvania state troopers nabbed 110,638 car drivers, 24,218 commercial vehicle operators, and 186 bus operators during this time period. Then again in June of 1976, on the Interstates alone the troopers issued citations to 1,611 commercial vehicle operators and 6,349 to private automobile drivers.

With the establishment of the national 55 mile-per-hour speed limit on a permanent basis, Section 107 of the Federal-Aid Highway Amendment of 1974, 23 U.S. 141, designated State enforcement certification as a continuing prerequisite for the approval of federal-aid highway projects. It also indirectly gave the states a mandate to rake in as much money as they can from speeding citations. In fact, it goes deeper than this and becomes more serpentine. Many police agencies utilize federal grants to purchase their radiopositioning equipment.

Another new wrinkle is the tandem radar units. Here's how this little trick works. Police establish a radar speed trap which is openly visible to passing motorists. This is done to give the drivers a false sense of security and to dupe them into accelerating once they feel that they are safely past the unit. But a few hundred feet down the highway and around the bend, a second radar unit is set up to ambush the unsuspecting cars.

Here's another gimmick the cops are using to entrap drivers. Police are installing radar units in unmarked cars which are pulled off on the side of the roadway and made to appear disabled by lifting the hood. They usually are parked facing oncoming traffic. Then the so-called disabled car clocks the passing motorists and a chase car farther down the road and out of sight picks them up like flies.

Some states are no longer giving a 5-to-10-mph grace range. Tickets are being issued for an infraction of just a few miles over the posted limits. Nevertheless, this book of mine will give you a few ideas about just how radar violations can be defended on the highways and in the courts. Citizens need no longer be intimidated by fast-talking cops and snappy looking electronic equipment.

One fine example of a man who fought back was cited by *Time*. Paul VanderMaat was clocked at 8 miles-per-hour over the speed limit in Los Alamos, New Mexico. However, he swore that he was driving no faster than the posted speed limit, 25 mph. Furious about the citation, he went home and consulted some books and a few weeks afterward explained to Judge Raymond E. Hunter that he had been nabbed about 10 minutes before a thunderstorm, just when the oncoming electricity creates ionized particles in the air that can throw a radar unit out of kilter. The verdict? Case dismissed!

We can thank Uncle Sam for the 55 mile-per-hour nationwide speed limits, and, therefore, indirectly for the widespread use and misuse of radiopositioning equipment. But he may not be finished with America's drivers yet.

Several members of the National Highway Traffic Safety Administration have voiced opinions that rules should be adopted which place a 95 mph ceiling on the overall speed capabilities of *all* cars, trucks, and motorcycles, save police and emergency vehicles. In addition, these same people would like to see car speedometers be numbered no higher than 85 mph and that at speeds greater than this the cars would be designed so that horns would beep and flasher lights would engage.

As if this type of involuntary restraint would not be enough, the National Transportation Safety Board has recommended that the top speed ability of cars be no more than the nation's highest legal speed limit.

There are two major arguments against these proposals. In the first place, a car must have energy in reserve to pass and escape certain situations. And then there is a matter of cost.

Road & Track stated that such speed-control systems

might add $25 to the cost of a vehicle and asks whether "a 4 percent possible reduction in traffic fatalities is worth $250,000,000 per year?" The magazine further contends that building a car with a maximum 55 mile-per-hour speed would cost more than building one that can go 125 mph.

And there is one point that has been raised by Dr. Ronald S. Morris, director of a driver research project at Texas A & M University, and that is that the 55 mile-per-hour speed limit may help increase the number of accidents because of the added stress it puts on drivers who feel relaxed at 70 mph.

When he requested 18 student safety researchers to "find a speed which is most comfortable to maintain" in vehicles with a masked off speedometer, the average speed came in at 70 mph. The speeds were recorded automatically by recorders hidden in the back seats so that the drivers would not be aware of the measurement exercise.

"Our data resulted in an overall mean comfortable speed of 70 mph. Some drivers were only comfortable at 77 mph," Dr. Morris told an interviewer. "It is reasonable to conclude that people are not comfortable driving at 55 miles-per-hour."

Dr. Morris feels that the sizeable gap between what the federal government says is the legal speed and what his drivers felt were comfortable speeds is great. The constant braking of the car's speed, and watching the speedometer, causes fatigue and stress, according to the doctor.

Dr. Morris concludes that "the additional stress can lead to exposure to greater accident hazards. And further, the constant throttle correction will result in poor engine performance and efficiency."

Unfortunately, the people who write and enforce the

laws haven't caught up with the most recent scientific data. For now we're stuck with the 55 mile-per-hour limit and with the legal establishment determined to enforce it. In the "Battle of the Cops vs. the Drivers," the cops have some powerful weapons, the most powerful of which is radar.

On February 14, 1977, the Comptroller General of the United States issued his Report to Congress (CED-77-27) entitled, "SPEED LIMIT 55, Is It Achievable?"

The report points out that the nation's motorists do not think that the fuel savings or the safety benefits of driving slower are worth the inconveniences.

The report states: "Increased enforcement nationwide has resulted in more speeding citations issued, but has not produced overall speed reductions since 1974. In view of states' other enforcement priorities and limited resources, additional state emphasis on speed limit enforcement could adversely affect other state needs. In addition, some state enforcement agencies believe several aspects of the 55 mph speed limit have contributed to the growing disrespect for laws and law enforcement officials.

"In 1975 about half of the states reported more drivers exceeding the 55 mph speed limit than complying with it. This puts a much larger burden on enforcement agencies than they had when speed limits were set so that only 15 percent of drivers exceeded the limits. State enforcement agencies said that too many drivers exceed the speed limit for them to enforce it effectively."

The Safety Administration reports that roughly 25 percent of its enforcement funding to the states is used to enforce the 55 mph speed limit—about $2.5 billion spent annually for police traffic services.

The report further says that, "state enforcement agencies have tried various speed enforcement techniques such as disguising their cars, cruising in teams, utilizing sophisticated new radar units, and trying other techniques. The result has been an increase in speeding arrests from 4 million in 1973 to 6 million in 1974 to over 7 million in 1975. In spite of these efforts more drivers are violating the 55 mph speed limit than violated previous speed limits.

"State enforcement agencies have many duties in addition to enforcing speed limits, such as assisting at traffic accidents, quieting local disturbances, apprehending intoxicated drivers, assisting stranded motorists, checking for illegal drugs, and patrolling high-accident locations. Since enforcement resources are limited, increasing emphasis on one responsibility reduces resources available for other responsibilities. Although state officials recognize the need for speed enforcement, they said that some of their other responsibilities require a higher priority for their limited resources.

"State officials explained that many of the higher speed roads, particularly interstate highways, have lower accident rates than secondary roads. They said that one of their high priority efforts is to patrol where the accidents are happening, which means patrolling secondary roads. However, state officials said that if they emphasize enforcement on secondary roads to combat accidents, speeds increase on the interstate and primary highways."

And what does the average motorist feel about all this? A study conducted in President Carter's State of Georgia tells it all.

BENEFIT OF 55 MPH SPEED LIMIT	PERCENT AGREED
Saves lives	72
Saves gas	70
Reduces accidents	68

The GAO report, at the same time showed that speed monitoring in Georgia recorded the following percentages of vehicles exceeding the 55 mph speed limit:

PERIOD	PERCENTAGE EXCEEDING 55 MPH
Year ended 9-30-75	62
Quarter ended 12-31-75	56
Quarter ended 3-31-76	66
Quarter ended 6-30-76	69

The report concluded: "It appears that speeding is similar in a way to smoking; people know it can be hazardous to their health, but they do it anyway."

Copies of GAO reports are available to the general public at a cost of $1.00 a copy. There is no charge for reports furnished to Members of Congress and congressional staff members. Officials of federal, state, and local governments may receive up to 10 copies free of charge. Members of the press, college libraries, faculty members, and students, and non-profit organizations may receive up to two copies free of charge.

Requesters entitled to this report without charge should address their request to:

U.S. General Accounting Office
Distribution Section, Room 4522
441 G St., NW
Washington, D.C. 20548

Requesters who are required to pay for the report should send their requests with cheques or money orders to:

U.S. General Accounting Office
Distribution Section
P.O. Box 1020
Washington, D.C. 20013

Be sure and cite on each order the following information: Report to Congress, CED-77-27, February 14, 1977.

The deck is not totally stacked in favor of the police. There are a *great many* things a smart driver can do to prepare himself. However, nothing in this book should be construed to mean that I advocate anyone's breaking the law. This book is designed to provide my fellow motorists with the guidance and information needed to fight against the unethical and often illegal speed traps being used, and, at the same time, provide motorists with the knowledge needed to obtain their full rights as a U.S. citizen, in both the courts of law and on the highways.

A wise man once said: "Constant vigilance is the price of liberty."

This I firmly believe. And I also believe that an informed public is a vigilant public.

CHAPTER 2

What Is Radar?

Radar is an acronym derived from the first letters of the phrase "radio detecting and ranging." Periodic radio wave pulses of very high voltage but short duration sent out from a powerful radar transmitter are reflected by objects within range of the radar unit. A small portion of the radiating energy bounces back as an echo to the radar receiver, via an antenna, which is most often at the transmitter site. The individual properties of the relayed echo are utilized to structure a picture or figure out the specific properties of the object which caused the echo.

Radar devices have been in use since the early 1950s. But even before its introduction, drivers had to contend with the white-gloved motorcycle cop hidden in a stand of trees or behind a billboard and the unnoticed hoses laid out across major thoroughfares. The rubber hoses, laid about 15 feet apart, operated on a time/distance gauge system. Once a vehicle triggered an initial switch that started the measurement, there was no way to turn back. While it was a burden and a bore to police officers assigned such duty, getting out of such citations for speeding was not that easy. The cops had a pretty fool-proof case based upon this system. In some ways, our modern electronic circuitry gives drivers a better chance to escape conviction.

Radiopositioning Equipment (Police Traffic Radar)

The principle behind police radiopositioning devices is the well-known *Doppler* effect. Christian Johann Doppler, an Austrian physicist and mathematician, discovered that if the distance is changing between an observer and a source of constant vibrations, as of light and sound, the wave number appears to be greater or less than the true value accordingly, as the distance is diminished or lengthened.

A good example of the "Doppler Slide" is the changing pitch of a train whistle heard by a listener near a railroad crossing. The pitch changes because of the relative motion between sound source and listener. As it pertains to radar, the principle states that radio waves reflected from a moving object will undergo a change in frequency in concert with the velocity of said moving target.

As the signal emitted from the speed trap radar device hits a passing vehicle and is immediately reflected back toward the antenna, the monitored car becomes a mobile transmitter. If the car is moving in the direction of the transmitter, the frequency will be higher when emitted; if it is moving away, the frequency will be lower. However, since the electronic system only gauges the *deviation* from the transmitted frequency without reference to motion, it makes no difference which direction the target is moving. A frequency variation of 31.4 cyles-per-second is equated to a velocity of one mile-per-hour. Therefore, a car moving either toward or away from the speed trap antenna at 100 miles-per-hour would cause a shift in frequency of 3,140 cps. This shift would be automatically translated by the speed meter and displayed on a cathode-ray tube screen or on a recorded strip chart.

Signals

Most military radar is pulse radar. These units emit short, very intense bursts or pulses of energy with relatively long gaps between bursts. The receiving unit receives echoes from the closest targets soon after the transmission of the burst, from targets at intermediate range a bit later, and from the most extreme targets at the termination of the interpulse interval. The cycle repeats itself as soon as enough time has passed to allow the reception of echoes from the farthest targets.

Police radiopositioning traffic devices use the Doppler effect with a continuous wave signal transmission. *It is nowhere nearly as selective as pulse radar.* Thus, rather than having a burst of energy home in on a target, the continuous wave signal device awaits the motion of a car entering its field of coverage to disturb the waves and send back a registration.

Today's electronic radar hands out tickets easily, conveniently, impersonally, and quickly. One company is even coming out with a unit that can take the vehicle's photograph (clearly showing the people in the front seat), record on the same card the speed limits, the extent of violation, the weather, time of day, and road conditions, as well as literally mailing it to you. The photographic angle may be construed as an invasion of privacy—imagine a married man out for a drive with his girlfriend; he is recorded speeding through a trap, and a photo-citation arrives at home to be opened by his wife.

But radar is not foolproof and every day drivers are beating the bleep in a number of ways on the highways and in the courts.

Non-Radar Devices

Outlawed in many states as illegal entrapment, the VASCAR speed gauge system marks the velocity of a moving car by recording the vehicle over a premeasured portion of roadway. VASCAR is merely an electronic time/distance computer.

Each driver must check with state and local governments to see if VASCAR is legal in his region. However, I can tell you that one state, New York, has installed more than 500 of these computers in its state police cruisers and in excess of 2,000 troopers have been trained and certified on them as qualified operators.

VASCAR is an acronym derived from the first letters of the phrase, "visual average speed computer and recorder." VASCAR is a trade name.

The VASCAR speed computer contains two main parts; the control module with its number display read out panel, and the computer module in the flat metal box which sits on the floor of the patrol car.

Once the trooper feeds the time and distance into the computer module, the velocity of the target vehicle is instantly flashed onto the read out panel. These numbers will remain in view until the computer is disengaged, cleared, and made ready for the next check.

VASCAR permits the trooper to make speed checks from a myriad of positions—parked along the highway, following another car, approaching oncoming vehicles from ahead or behind, and even at intersections when a vehicle might speed past the trooper's position.

However, it is essential when making a speed check that two reference points, the primary point situated where the clocking starts and the secondary where the clocking ends, be employed. Almost anything can be used as a reference point, e.g., a crack in the highway, the shadow of a distant tree, a road sign or any other easily identifiable point. These points of reference must be at least a tenth of a mile apart and are more often close to a half mile.

So that you'll better understand it, let's look at an example of how VASCAR might be employed.

Assume a trooper is tailing a suspected speeder. As the target car arrives at the primary reference point, the trooper flips on the time toggle switch. When the trooper reaches the same spot in his car the distance toggle switch is engaged. The time switch is then closed as the target vehicle reaches a second reference point and the distance switch is flipped down when the trooper reaches it. With this information, the computer now has all it needs to calculate the target vehicle's speed. It results in a read-out of the average speed over the measured distance rather than the peak speed.

New York State takes great care to make sure its troopers know what they are doing. All officers must certify as qualified on VASCAR before they are permitted to use it in actual situations. Their training includes classroom instruction followed by three weeks of practice on the highways. After two weeks, a supervisor is assigned to ride with the pupil trooper and see if any further training and/or guidance is needed. One week later the trooper is expected to make a series of 30 practice checks against free-flow highway traffic while a supervisor, in another vehicle, makes similar confirmations. If the checks of the trainee and the checks submitted by the instructor are largely correspondent the trooper is certified.

The accuracy of the computer must be checked before the start of every tour by the operator. If it is not accurate then there is a calibrating screw on the control module with which the device can be aligned.

VASCAR is not a replacement for radar, but it can be used in certain situations when radar is not suitable due to conditions. It does away with the need for high-speed pursuits since the patrol car does not have to keep pace with the target vehicle to obtain a reading. And the trooper can take it easy when pulling over the alleged offender since the numbers will remain on the display until the officer erases the computer's memory.

VASCAR has several limitations.

1. There is a percentage of error innate in its circuitry.
2. Many states have already outlawed such devices.
3. Police operators must be highly trained and skilled at using the speed meters.

Orbis

Developed by Ling-Temco-Vought, this is an experimental system that utilizes a camera to record speed limit violations. A series of ORBIS monitoring units are set apart on a highway area. Cars passing by are automatically measured for speed. If their velocity is in excess of the posted limitations, a motor-driven 35mm SLR camera with a 250mm telephoto lens snaps a picture of the car and driver 35 milliseconds after the switch is engaged.

An infrared sensitive film stock (ASA 4500 is available to DOT already), and a specialized 200 watt-second strobe light with filters provides enough illumination for nocturnal photography. Windshield reflection is eased by a special polarizing filter. The black-and-white picture shows the car's front section, the license plate if there is one, and the driver's face. Superimposed on the lower section of the photograph are the time and date of the alleged infraction and the speed limit as well as the recorded speed of the vehicle and its location. Like the previously mentioned device that utilizes a camera, the question of invasion of privacy crops up again. This is such a serious concern that the Department of Transportation in Washington, D.C. was considering recording commuter trends (number of riders in cars) by photographic testimony until this query was introduced. No firm decision has been made yet.

Whether an unmanned camera's photograph will stand as *prima facie* evidence in a court of law is questionable anyway. Banks are up against the same problem with their remote cameras. Videotape of a bank robbery is not sufficient evidence alone to convict an alleged stick-up man. Fingerprints and/or visual identification from a witness is also demanded by the courts today. Nevertheless, *Motor Trend* has reported that at least 30 speeding convictions have been based upon ORBIS photography alone. However, these cases have been heard only in magistrate courts. *Motor Trend* also reported that the National Highway Traffic Safety Administration (DOT) is one of the parties in America most interested in this new device. So if they can get around the questions I've raised here, we may have another trap to figure out a countermeasure for because it is bound to be misused.

I like radar as a valid deterrent against reckless and drunken drivers and to combat the habitual speeder. What bothers me is that there are many more drivers who obey the speed limits than do not, and, therefore, the percentages are not in favor of those motorists who rarely break the posted limits. The speed demons get away in most cases while the usually careful drivers get caught a few miles over to help fill some quota program. *And,* the police are not trained enough in the esoteric complexities and theory of radar. All police radar operators are expected to know is how to engage, calibrate, and read the electronic devices.

A Pennsylvania law enforcement officer related to me that the training he received on his radar unit was most superficial and inadequate. It comprised of reading a brochure the manufacturer had published and a quick talk by the force's radio technician. When he asked for additional information and training, his superior told him: "Look, do your best and try to stay out of court."

CHAPTER 3

Defensive Driving

The best way not to get caught by police radar is not to speed. However, considering the design of today's super highways and the power of the automobiles, this is ofttimes easier said than done. The federal government is not developing 55-mph roadways, and the car manufacturers make their acceleration systems so that a motorist's foot need only slightly depress the pedal to hit high speeds. For example, when you are traveling at 55-mph, the gas pedal needs only to be knocked down another inch to hit 70-mph and two to surpass 80-mph.

Defensive driving is the key and the measures below may be of help to you.

Electronic Countermeasures

Electronic countermeasures (ECM) is the technique of nullifying, delimiting, or disturbing the utilization of electromagnetic-wave propagation (radar) for monitoring target objectives. *For every measure depending upon electromagnetic-wave propagation, there is a countermeasure,* allowed the time and funding to discover it. In turn, for every countermeasure, a counter-countermeasure can be found. This endless sequence is limited only by man's invention, creativity, and knowledge of application.

Electronic countermeasures can be classified as: *Detection:* radar warning systems; *Deception:* passive reflectors, absorbing material, chaff, transponders; and *Denial:* jammers, chaff.

DETECTION

Radar Warning Systems. There are many passive radar warning devices on the market today. Since 1974 sales of these microwave radar detectors have quadrupled. The manufacturers estimate that during 1977 their sales will double again to approximately $100 million at the retail level.

Between the use of Citizens Band radios and radar warning devices, a full-scale war has broken out between drivers and law enforcement agencies involved in highway speed control. It has been reported that in 1976 over 500,000 radar detection devices were sold. And one industry representative predicts that by 1980 there will be in excess of 8 million in use.

WARNING: *The use of such detection devices may be regulated by state or local laws, and, therefore, it is best to check out your driving areas prior to purchasing one.*

The State of Oklahoma in the first Session of its 36th Legislature (1977) introduced a bill (House Bill No. 1089) that would not only prohibit the use of radar detectors in motor vehicles but would also prohibit the advertising, sale, or distribution of such devices. While this bill might change slightly in its wording by the time it gets through committee, it read as follows when introduced.

BE IT ENACTED BY THE PEOPLE OF THE STATE OF OKLAHOMA:

SECTION 1. A. It shall be unlawful for any person to operate a motor vehicle upon any road, street, highway, or turnpike of this state when such vehicle is equipped with any radar detection device or mechanism to detect the emission of radio microwaves in the electromagnetic spectrum, which microwaves, commonly referred to as radar, are employed by police or the Oklahoma Highway Patrol to measure the speed of motor vehicles upon any road, street, highway, or turnpike of this state for law enforcement purposes.

B. It shall be unlawful to use any such device or mechanism upon any such motor vehicle upon any road, street, highway, or turnpike.

C. It shall be unlawful to advertise the sale of, be in possession of, sell or distribute any such device or mechanism in this state.

D. Any person violating any provision of this section shall be fined not less than Fifty Dollars ($50.00) nor more than Two Hundred Dollars ($200.00) or be sentenced to not less than thirty (30) days nor more than six (6) months in a county jail, or both.

SECTION 2. The presence of any such prohibited device or mechanism in or upon a motor vehicle upon any road, street, highway, or turnpike of this state shall constitute a *prima facie* evidence of the violation of Section 1 of this act. The state or any political subdivision thereof need not prove that the device or mechanism in question was in operative condition or being operated.

SECTION 3. All devices or mechanisms prohibited in Section 1 of this act are deemed contraband and shall be seized and summarily forfeited to a peace officer of this state.

All such devices or mechanisms seized or surrendered under the provisions of this act shall be destroyed after all legal actions have been exhausted. The destruction shall be done under the supervision of the Commissioner of the Department of Public Safety in a manner best determined to render the property totally useless and unrepairable. A permanent record of all property destroyed under the provisions of this act shall be maintained by the Commissioner of the Department of Public Safety.

SECTION 4. The provisions of Section 1 of this act shall not apply to:

1. Any receiver of radio waves of any frequency lawfully licensed by any state or federal agency; or

2. Motor vehicles owned by the state or any political subdivision thereof and which are used by the police of any such government, nor to the law enforcement officers in their official duties, nor to the sale of any such device or mechanism to law enforcement agencies for their use in their official duties.

SECTION 5. Sections 1 through 4 of this act shall be codified in the Oklahoma Statutes as Sections 11-808 through 11-811 of Title 47, unless the same shall create a duplication in numbering.

SECTION 6. It being immediately necessary for the presentation of the public peace, health, and safety, an emergency is hereby declared to exist, by reason whereof this act shall take effect and be in full force from and after its passage and approval.

In the State of Michigan during the month of January, 1977, Michigan State Police Lansing Post Commander Lt. Richard Abbott is reported to have told his officers that they should confiscate any radar detection devices found in private cars, hold them for evidence, and issue appropriate tickets on the spot. According to *The State Journal,* this action was attempted on the basis of a 1929 state law banning police radio monitors in private cars.

Then in a test case, Judge Ronald Taylor, Berrien County District Court, ruled that this law does not apply to the radar units. On January 24 it was reported in *The State Journal* that Col. Forrest Jacob, deputy director of the state police, told his officers not to make any more arrests for the use of the receivers.

This case is now on its way to the higher courts. And while the decision only applies within Berrien County now, the judge's legal reasoning is affecting actions elsewhere in the state. In fact, prosecutors and police across the state have, in several instances, dropped charges against motorists charged for using the detectors.

One vital question the courts must ask is: Is a radar detection device a police radar monitor or an amateur radio band monitor that has the capabilities to be nonselective enough to pick up police frequencies?

Let's use this Michigan situation as a further example of interpretation. If the radar detector is, in fact, a police monitor, it is illegal in private cars (without special permits) under the 1929 state law.

If the device is defined as an actual amateur radio receiver, then federal law would seem to cover it. Remember that it is federal law and not state law that exercises jurisdiction over radio waves.

Another legal question arises over the use of the frequencies allocated for police radar. Since the police agencies merely "share" these frequencies with other users and services, it is not theirs exclusively. Does the fact that they happen to be working on it make it automatically a police frequency?

Many police forces now operate CB radios in their cars. Does the fact that the police have and operate these radios make CB a "police" frequency?

The laws are not always directed at the actual use of

detection devices. Many communities make use of a loophole in the law that states something like: *nothing besides the rearview mirror may be on the windshield or obstructing the front field-of-view.* In the Commonwealth of Pennsylvania this law has been used to cite people for improper placement of state inspection stickers and for toys that hang about the rearview mirror stem. *So they can get you if they want to.*

The following states are those that do not, presently, allow detection devices: Virginia, West Virginia, New Jersey, Connecticut, and Washington, D.C.

Naturally, the outlawing of radar detectors by these states (and others in the future) is bad for the manufacturers. One of the nation's largest, Electrolert, has retaliated by launching a massive campaign to combat the new laws. In the state of Virginia, it is called the "Virginia Fuzzbuster Brigade." Co-sponsored by *Overdrive Magazine,* 15,000 cardboard imitation Fuzzbusters were produced for distribution via truckstops. An additional 25,000 are being distributed throughout other trouble states.

Posters announcing the campaign said, "Get your bear-bait free. Mount it and let the 'bears who bite' get a mouthful of cardboard!"

According to Electrolert president Dale Smith, his firm has already invested approximately $150,000 in litigation in the state of Virginia alone. The law in Virginia has been on the books since 1962.

I have heard reports that state troopers have entered trucks and cars to remove detectors without permission. *Remember!* Trespass, in its most comprehensive sense, signifies any transgression or offense against the law of nature, of society, or of the country in which we live, and holds true whether it relates to a man's personal property or to his person. *Trespass quare clausum fregit.* This is the commonlaw action for damages for an unlawful entry or trespass upon a plaintiff's land or vehicle.

LIMITATIONS

Remember! These devices are not foolproof. They pick up all kinds of signals, e.g., military, airport, and scientific radar. *False readings are common.* Most of the devices just have too wide a frequency range.

One manufacturer recognizes these limitations and now sells (as of 10/1/76) two filters that will help get rid of most of the false signals picked up by its Snooper units. One is placed in the power cord and eliminates false signals caused by transmitting a CB radio in or close to the vehicle. According to the manufacturer, another filter inside the unit eliminates most other false signals. The cost is $15.00 at the time of this writing.

Some detection devices come pre-wired with a cigarette lighter adapter. However, this adapter does not fit well into all cars, and even though the pilot light may glow, the unit may still lack sufficient receiving power. The radar detection device may suffer damage as a result of this poor connection.

DEVICES

1. **Radar Sentry,** produced by Radatron, Inc., North Tonawanda, New York, is one of the most popular units. A miniature, transistorized, electronic microwave detector, it is completely self-contained. The unit is composed of two conical chambers, and it is highly responsive to both "X" band (10,525 GHz) horizontally and vertically polarized speed meters.

The manufacturer states that the detector will give a range of one-half mile. Cost: $49.95.

2. **Bear Hunter,** manufactured by Universal Machine Company, Inc., Communications Products Division, 2300 Reagan Street, Dallas, Texas 75219, sports both visual and audible (switchable) signals, but is different from many other detectors in a very important way. It utilizes a horn type antenna with exactly tuned cavities to eliminate much of the false triggering common to detectors.

The unit's dual band covers two radar bands: "X" band (10,525 GHz) and "K" band (24,150 GHz). The operator need not switch from one band to another; the unit is totally automatic. It comes with two different mountings: (A) pedestal for dash mounting, and (B) a mounting that glues to the windshield.

The manufacturer claims that the unit is good up to 5 miles. Cost: $149.95

3. **Fuzzbuster,** Manufactured by Electrolert, Troy, Ohio 45373, has sold over 300,000 units to date. The firm claims that the key to the unit's effectiveness is that it will always see the radar six times as far as the radar can see you and in some cases, ten times as far. Therefore, unless you're going 120 miles-per-hour and the police have their beam straight across the highway, you will have more than sufficient time to react and slow down.

This unit is so sensitive that the company claims it will trigger on a signal a thousand times less than that used by a Citizens Band radio. They say it will trigger on 0.01 microvolt. It's said to be between 12 and 18 dB more sensitive than an F-4 fighter's fire control radar. The technology is so highly specialized for this unit that the manufacturer produces its own microwave diode detectors to meet their own standards.

Fuzzbuster adapts to positive or negative ground vehicles. It has an audio cueing system that announces radar lock-on with a short beep. Its visual indicator may be used to find out where the radar is located and what type of trap is being entered. It is said to be effective against the new moving radar.

In free space it can lock-in on radar up to eight miles away, according to the manufacturer. Cost: $79.00-90.00.

4. **Senturion,** also available from Radatron, Inc., 2424 Niagara Falls Blvd., North Tonawanda, New York 14120, detects moving radar and speed gun, plus "standard" traffic control radar. According to John Gambino, president, last year Senturion accounted for about $5 million in sales. He feels that in 1977 this figure will double.

This unit offers visual and audible warning signals, integrated circuitry, a computer designed horn antenna, dual mounting brackets, a die cast metal case, 12 volt operation—connects to the car's ignition—positive or negative ground, and an automatic noise limiter.

The unit claims maximum sensitivity and long range. Cost: $79.95

5. **Bearfinder** is produced in Sydney, Ohio. It can operate from a direct battery connection or plugged into the cigarette lighter's socket. Like all such detectors, it drains very little from the battery (about as much as an electric clock—200 milliamps).

This unit is a favorite of many long-haul truckers. The dual signal, visual and audible, can operate separately. Therefore, on night trips when a partner driver is sleeping in the cab, the unit will emit only a visual signal if it is so set, and in this way not wake up the passenger. On the other hand, during the day, when the sunlight might make the visual signal hard to read, the unit's horn issues a bleeping report.

Another feature is its mounting. It adheres to the dash

with Velcro material to allow easy removal. The manufacturer calls this "Bear Claws." In this way it can be hidden quickly from police and be removed when parking so that thieves will not be tempted by the device.

The manufacturer claims the device has a range of one-half to 2.5 miles. Cost: $89.95-109.95.

6. **The Snooper** is manufactured by Autotronics, Inc., P.O. Box 31433, Dallas, Texas 75231. This device mounts on the dashboard, windshield, or similar location that affords a clear view of the roadway ahead. According to *Hi-Performance Cars,* April, '73, ". . . near perfect radar has a calibrated range of 936 feet. The Snooper has a calibrated range of 3,520 feet." The Snooper was first put on the market in 1972. Cost: $79.95.

7. **The Super Snooper,** a spin-off by Autotronics, Inc., of its Snooper, is able to receive signals from both "K" band and the conventional "X" band radar units. The "K" band units are more powerful than the "X" band units. Yet they are becoming very popular with police because of their portability not their range. Many hand-held radar units operate on this band. All the officer has to do is point it as he would a pistol, and he'll receive a read-out instantly. Cost: $179.95.

It has been estimated that an average of five radar units per police force are in operation in over 80 percent of the nation's cities. And for many Americans, especially long haul truckers and on-the-road salesmen, profit and loss is directly related to the ability to travel fast between several ground points. Radar detectors help make this possible. They are here to stay.

While it is impossible to recommend one radar detector over another because of variables like driving terrain, dashboard and windshield designs, types of radar in use at a particular trap, etc., there are several facts about radar detection one must keep in mind.

First, police radar equipment will operate at its greatest range on long, level straightaways. However, the greater the distance ofttimes the worse it is for the officer responsible for reading the speeds. Since the operator *must* have visual observation of the vehicle he is tracking, it does not do him much good to be able to pick up a moving target three miles away. At a distance of more than 1,700 feet the human depth of perception will not allow for positive identification if the speeding vehicle is situated within a pack. And once in a court of law, the police officer will have to swear, under oath, that he could clearly make out the target vehicle as being out in front, alone, closest to the radar device when the reading was issued.

Most police officers realize this and, therefore, concentrate on vehicles within a 1,000 to 2,000 foot range so that they will be able to make a solid case in court.

Police radar cannot detect speeders from around curves, through stands of trees, or over buildings and hills. On the other hand, a good radar detector will be able to pick up scattered energy from a police radar unit that is out of view. This scattering happens when the radar signal hits a barrier and portions of the signal break away into the atmosphere.

Regardless of the radar warning system selected, there are certain facts and figures that every driver must realize.

1. The power output of police radar is approximately 50mW–100mW.
2. The distance at which speed meters can clock are:
   Short Range: 150 feet
   Medium Range: 200–900 feet
   Long Range: 1000–1500 feet

THE AVERAGE STOPPING DISTANCE OF A CAR ON DRY HIGHWAY*

VELOCITY (MPH)	DISTANCE BEFORE YOUR FOOT TOUCHES BRAKE	DISTANCE BEFORE COMPLETE STOP
30	33 ft.	78 ft.
40	44 ft.	125 ft.
50	55 ft.	188 ft.
60	66 ft.	272 ft.
70	77 ft.	381 ft.

*Pavement

DECEPTION

Passive Reflectors. Special shaping of bodies that can reduce a target's cross section (the area of the target that effectively returns echoes to the transmitter) have been molded in attempts to beat radar. Other similar ECM (Electronic Countermeasures) aids have been corner reflectors and Luneberg lenses, which concentrate the energy they reflect back to the radar gun in such a way that it produces a false reading.

Absorbing Material. It has been reported that some people have gone to the extent of spray painting their vehicle's exterior with Echo-sorb. This is expensive but it works. Echo-sorb is the paint used by the military to insulate radar labs because it will not reflect radar signals.

Chaff. The use of chaff dates back to the Royal Air Force raid on Hamburg in 1943, and is one of the oldest techniques for totally confusing radar signals.

Chaff are metallic strips pre-cut to lengths resonant at a specific radar frequency so that they return wide radar echoes to the emitter unit. These echoes confuse the radar operator by generating false targets or din on the screen, demanding the operator take time to analyze and sort out the true from the false images. It can also screen or mask the actual oncoming vehicle so that the radar operator is unable to detect its presence. Or it can enable a vehicle being tracked to break track.

The design of chaff which the British called "window," the Americans "chaff," and the Germans "Dueppel," is a complicated function and involves factors such as the desired radar cross section and frequency coverage. For coverage at the lower frequencies, where longer wavelengths demand longer strands of chaff, Lundy Electronics developed what is called "resilient" chaff, a bundle of some twenty coated and uncoated fibers entwined and bonded together.

Certain aircraft have chaff dispensers as self-protecting measures. Also, on occasion, military aircraft have seeded vast air corridors with chaff during an air strike to disrupt enemy tracking devices. Packages of chaff are automatically torn open upon release, and their contents blossom into mini cloud formations within the aircraft's slipstream. Chaff has also been dispersed by chaff-dispensing rockets fired well ahead of bombers to ensure that an ample curtain of diversion will effect prior to the hit at the strike zone.

Lundy Electronics is a principal manufacturer of aluminum glass chaff. Owens-Corning Fiberglass Corp. also makes metalized glass chaff. Revere Copper and Glass has explored the properties of nylon glass chaff.

Motorists have been known to employ this method against police radar. There are several ways this is done. The most popular way is to place balls of tinfoil under hub caps and wheel covers. The bouncing and reverberating of the metal globes emits sounds resonant at a specific radar frequency. This can also occur when balls of tinfoil are placed in other cavities within the car's bodywork.

One man I met took the same principle a step further.

He keeps a key ring around the rearview mirror and insists that the high-pitched reports caused by the meeting of keys makes the radar ineffective. I have no proof that this works; however, the concept is noteworthy.

In Chapter 8 I will list the state police frequencies for all 50 states, Guam, and Puerto Rico. Local, county, turnpike, and campus police force allocated frequencies, etc., are available to you also but could not be listed herein because of space limitations.

Transponders. These devices are transmitter-receivers, capable of accepting the challenge of an interrogator and automatically transmitting an appropriate answer. Transponders can return to the original tracking radar an overall fixed time delay, thereby causing an inaccurate reading and confusion.

DENIAL

Jamming. Deception-jamming techniques are based upon the concept of working on pulse beats received from a radar unit so that the re-radiated signal from the target will mislead the radar operators.

Jamming signals is not legal. However, the equipment necessary to jam signals may be bought and sold openly since the gear has other uses.

Sweep Jamming. This is a jamming of a radarscope by sweeping the spectrum of radar-beam coverage with high speed electromagnetic waves having the same frequency waves as those received by the radarscope. This procedure produces a series of bursts that masks incoming signals.

Sweep Generators. These are electronic circuits that generate a voltage current, usually repeating, at a prescribed rate. The emitted waveform is utilized as a time base to then be directed at the deflection system of the radar unit's electro-beam gun.

There are four types of sweep generators available.

1. Linear sweep generators
2. Circular sweep generators
3. Rotating radial sweep generators
4. Hyperbolic sweep generators

White-noise Jamming. One of the most popular forms of ECM, this procedure produces synthetic noises that cause reverberation of the radar transmitter signal. It is simple and easy.

Where to Purchase Sweep Generators

One of the most complete catalogues I've been able to find for such instruments is put out in the form of sales bulletins by Lectronic Research Laboratories, Inc., Atlantic & Ferry Avenues, Camden, New Jersey 08104. Their telephone number is (609) 541-4200.

The firm claims to maintain a large and varied inventory of microwave components and equipment, laboratory grade test equipment, and precision components, spanning the entire spectrum from DC to microwave frequencies.

REMEMBER: Detection devices are not jammers.

Report any unusual interference your radio may experience to the nearest FCC field office for investigation. The complete listing and addresses may be found in Chapter 8.

CHAPTER 4

Citizens Band Radio

No book on police radar would be complete without the mention of Citizens Band radio, a medium around which America's newest and fastest-growing subculture congregates. To get in, you merely turn on a CB radio. To get out, you simply turn it off.

I have been using CB for over 12 years. In fact, when I originally had it, licenses were free and the transceiver could be left unguarded in open convertibles because no one would know what it was to steal it. But today's upswing in popularity was caused by the fuel crisis. Professional long-haul truckers, in an attempt to run their powerful machines at speeds over 55-mph which gives better gas mileage, purchased CB radios to advise each other of police radar traps. When the motoring public became aware of CB's existence and manifold uses, CB units wound up in campers, buses, airplanes, and handbags.

Today the Electronic Industries Association estimates that one out of every 22 vehicles on the road is CB-equipped. This figure included one out of 21 passenger cars, two out of five long-haul trucks, one out of seven recreational vehicles, and three out of seven four-wheel drive vehicles.

In an effort to foil the "smokey" reports being transmitted between private vehicles, state police forces started to equip their patrol cars with CB radios. Most states are at least 50 to 75 percent CB-equipped and, as far as I am able to tell, there may be only two states that do not permit CB radios in their official vehicles; Florida is one of these states. On the other hand, the State of Missouri, according to Col. Samuel S. Smith, Superintendent, Missouri State Highway Patrol, now operates 723 mobile units in their field cars and 27 base units in weigh stations and troop headquarters.

While many police departments consider Citizens Band radio an aid to law enforcement (during the first eleven months of a Missouri State Highway Patrol CB project, officers and base stations received a total of 92,896 CB reports; 16,703 or 17 percent were to report crimes or violations, thus resulting in 4,300 arrests), too many police forces still use the medium to trap drivers.

One common ploy is for the police officer to cruise up and down the highway giving false "smokey" reports when his partner is actually waiting nearby with a radar unit in place. The battle between "smokies" and motorists has become a free-for-all and anything seems to go—both ways. Drivers should be sure to confirm and re-confirm radar sightings and free-flow road conditions with other vehicles. Never take any report as the gospel.

A southern city, disgusted beyond endurance with CB-ers discovering its radar traps, built an electronic jamming station. Naturally, it became impossible to operate CB radios within a certain radius of this apparatus. It worked for a while. Then one day their jamming program was discovered and an aware CB-er alerted the Federal Communications Commission in Washington, D.C. It took immediate action against the community police force for operating an illegal jammer.

When I first started with CB radio, the FCC would monitor the bands on a regular basis and issue pink tickets (fines) for improper use of the medium. But today the very number of units in operation precludes this being done in such a concentrated way. Robert M. Booth, Jr., general counsel for the American Radio Relay League, in comments to the Federal Communications Commission on June 10, 1976, stated that "there is a possibility there will be 20 million units on the streets by the end of this year and usage ultimately will reach the 80-million figure in this country." And this inability of the FCC to properly enforce its rules and regulations works to the benefit of many policemen who choose to make illegal use of CB.

One local policeman I interviewed during the preparation of this book told me that his commander had requested several of his fellow officers to install CB radios in their patrol cars and circulate around town with the mikes keyed open onto a transistor radio blasting rock and roll music. In this way the "trucker's channels" would be jammed and unusable. Also, by continually moving, it was almost impossible for other CB-ers or the FCC to triangulate on them.

"This went on for several months and the kids never did figure it out. By the time we had finished, there wasn't a channel they could use," he related. "The only reason this jamming was called off was because between this new single sideband stuff and the 40 channels it became impossible to continue. The commander would have had to have every car involved."

This officer went on to tell me that the issuance of speeding citations escalated, the money rolled into city hall, and everyone was happy. In fact, the commander received a special departmental recognition for his precinct's outstanding conviction record in this area. "The fat cats in the grey suits were happier than ever," he continued. "But it was not long until the word got out inside the upper levels and the commander was relocated in another precinct."

Throughout the country, stories of police lashing out at CB-ers continue to appear. In the *Journal-Courier,* Hartford, Connecticut, it was reported that a motorist was arrested and fined $15 for using a CB radio while operating his car. Some police sources said there is a law (rarely enforced) which does prohibit those driving cars, not trucks, from using CB equipment while moving on the road.

Many police agencies can pull a law from their hip pockets similar to the one cited in Connecticut. When these regulations were originally passed and put on the books, they were for the purpose of controlling mobile telephone operations. It is still illegal in many states for drivers to talk via mobile telephones while operating a moving motor vehicle. The matter comes down to one of definition: What constitutes a mobile telephone? While it sounds absurd to think a police officer would even try pulling such a pinch, anything is possible.

A Michigan State Trooper suggested that, since the police are now "officially" on CB, it could be called a "police frequency," thus making every CB mobile in Michigan in technical violation of a law that says it is illegal to have police monitors in private cars.

Here's a classic attempt by police to put the arm on CB-ers. It shows just how far someone is willing to stretch a point. The case in question is *People of the State of Illinois* (plaintiff) vs. *Sammie J. Graham* (defendant). Mr. Graham was taken to court on a charge that he obstructed a peace officer by alerting fellow CB-ers about a radar trap via his Citizens Band radio unit. After both sides presented their arguments, the Livingston County judge handed down the following verdict.

"Freedom of speech is not absolute. Regulation as to time, place, and manner of such right is proper when reasonably related to a valid public interest." *See, Bridges vs. Davis,* 443 F Supp. 970 (1971). If one is engaged in criminal conduct, the First Amendment is not applicable; and, where one's otherwise lawful conduct is producing an imminent threat of uncontrollable violence or riot, police officers may interfere with a citizen's absolute freedom of speech. *See, United States vs. Borgese,* 235 F Supp. 286 (1964). *People vs. Meyer,* 44 Ill. 2d 1 (1969).

In the case at bar, did defendant Sammie Graham's verbal communication on a Citizens Band radio amount to criminal conduct, to wit, obstruction of a peace officer, so as to be unprotected by the Federal and State "Freedom of Speech" amendments? In, *People vs. Raby,* 40 Ill. 2d 392, 240 NE 2d 595, the court stated:

> "Obstruction means to be or to come in the way of . . . and (implies) some physical act or exertion. Given a reasonable and natural construction, (this) term does not proscribe mere argument with a policeman about the validity of an arrest or other police action, but proscribes only some physical act which imposes an obstacle which may impede, hinder, interrupt, prevent or delay the performance of the officer's duties, such as going limp, forcefully resisting or physically aiding a

third party to avoid arrest." *See also Landry vs. Daley,* 280 F Supp. 938, 959. (1968).

Under certain circumstances, a defendant can interfere with and obstruct an officer in the performance of his duties by verbal communication just as effectively as if he had touched or otherwise physically interfered with the officer. *See, People vs. Gibbs,* 253 NE 2d 121. However, the *Gibbs* case can be distinguished from the case at bar. In the *Gibbs* case, the police officers had stopped some disorderly youths and proceeded to search said youths when the defendant, in that case, appeared, advised the youths of their rights, and that a search without a warrant could be avoided if said youths entered a building, which said youths proceeded to do. In the instant case, there is no evidence nor is there any allegation that the police had confronted a violator of the law. The only allegation is that defendant Sammie Graham obstructed a police officer in monitoring traffic upon the highway. Defendant's conduct of communicating the location of the police officer could be obstruction of a police officer if the court were to assume that all or most drivers of automobiles proceeding along said highway were violating the law. It would be inappropriate for the court to make such an assumption.

This is a case of first impression and it is conceivable that similar communication under certain facts and circumstances could amount to obstruction of a peace officer. However, in the case at bar, the charge, as alleged, does not constitute conduct amounting to obstruction of a peace officer in violation of Ch 38 31-1 Ill. Rev. Stat.

It is Therefore Ordered, Adjudged, and Decreed that Defendant's Motion to Dismiss be and the same is granted. Cause is Ordered Dismissed.

DATED THIS 6TH DAY OF DECEMBER, 1976

This verdict was handed down in the Circuit Court of the Eleventh Judicial Circuit, Livingston County, State of Illinois. It was Case Number 76 CM 193. In Chapter 7 additional court cases will be discussed that might be of benefit in setting precedents in future court battles across the nation.

Before CB radio came on the scene, motorists would flash their headlights to warn each other of police speed traps. CB just makes it easier and more secure for the drivers, and, in turn, more frustrating for the police who must make quotas each period.

What Is CB?

Citizens Band (40 CB frequencies in the 27-MHz band) was established in 1947 by the FCC to permit personal, short-distance radio-communications by radio. It is freely available to any U.S. citizen, male or female and 18 years of age or older. Persons under 18 may operate CB transceivers under the supervision of a licensee who takes total responsibility and accountabilty for proper radio operation and conduct.

News! The FCC has changed the name of the Citizens Radio Service to the Personal Radio Service. And what was known as a Class D CB license is now known as Citizens Band (CB) Radio Service.

All the new rules were published in the December 23, 1976, issue of the *Federal Register* (available for $.75 from the U.S. Government Printing Office, Washington, D.C. 20402).

Is a License Required?

Yes. But, for the time being, there is *no* license fee! The FCC has jurisdiction over all radio transmission in the

United States. Before a transmitter can be placed on the air, a station license must be obtained from the Agency of the Federal Government. Most manufacturers include license applications with their units. A recent FCC ruling requires new sets to have a packet containing CB rules, a license application, and a temporary 60-day permit. The regular FCC Form 505 can be obtained from the Federal Communications Commission, Washington, D.C. 20554.

While that form is being processed you may broadcast using a temporary permit (FCC Form 555-B) which you fill out but do not mail in. This permit is good for 60 days from the date you mail in your regular application. It even provides for a temporary call sign for your CB radio station (the letter K plus the initials of your first and last name, plus your Zip Code number).

Police cannot ask to see your CB license! A friend in Mississippi told me about an experience he had with a local police officer harassing CB-ers at a truckstop. The policeman circulated among the cars parked in front of the restaurant and demanded to see FCC operating permits for CB rigs. Only the FCC can demand to see your license. Local police, or any police agency, for that matter, do not have any jurisdiction over broadcasting equipment, its use, misuse, or license procedures. It is the other way around; the FCC has enforcement powers over the police concerning the broadcasting equipment they utilize. And you would be surprised how many police forces do not abide by the letter of the law regulating its transceivers.

What Is the Maximum Range Possible with CB?

Range is determined by numerous factors, e.g., type of equipment, transmitting power, operating frequency, surrounding terrain, interference factors, type of antenna, the range between units, and antenna elevation. Cars should be able to communicate from 5 to 15 miles at full power with a good antenna; 10 to 20 miles between a base station and a mobile unit; and from 15 to 40 miles for fixed-base stations.

How Much Does a Transceiver Cost?

The Electronic Industries Association estimates that over $2.4 billion has been invested in CB equipment used by the American public. The old 23-channel mobile units cost between $119-129 at cheaper levels, $149-169 at mid-tag, and $199 and up for expensive models. However, since the introduction of 40-channel units, January 1, 1977, you should be able to cut these prices greatly now.

A one-step retailer will have a 35 percent margin built into his prices.

Which Unit Is the Best?

As you look at the different CB radios available on the market, keep in mind that unlike the conventional AM/FM radio, *all* Citizens Band radios must be type-approved by the FCC. This means that they must meet certain standards. Behind the cosmetics—fancy front panels, sporty meters, extra switches, odd-shaped mikes, and container designs—you can be confident that the equipment has been tested for frequency stability, performance capabilities under various weather conditions, operation under different voltage conditions, etc.

CB is a superb way to learn about upcoming radar traps. But range is a key factor in its effectiveness to alert you of what's going on ahead of and behind you.

Your range will be controlled greatly by the antenna

you select and where it is placed. Mobile antennae are styled for mounting on the rear fender, roof, trunk, or bumper. They are all basically the same—omnidirectional. The most common is the "whip." Usually it is mounted on the rear bumper, which is the *worst* place for it. It may be easier to install there, but it loses almost half its radiation efficiency. The best place for a mobile antenna is mid-roof or at least mid-trunk.

If you are willing to spend a few more dollars for a Single Sideband set, increasingly more popular among CB-ers, the distance available will more than double. Single Sideband suppresses the carrier signal before transmission so that all the power is concentrated within one sideband. These sets have less interference and greater maximum range. More important, it is doubtful that any police force has these units. First, they cost too much; and second, the police have probably only just finished buying the standard 23-channel equipment.

But for use on the highways against radar traps you are best off when operating units the "smokies" do not have: 40-channel sets and/or sideband sets. Transceivers are available which offer both together in a single unit.

Police with the conventional 23-channel rigs will only be able to monitor these channels. Smart drivers will jump upstairs to the higher channels and lose the uniformed eavesdroppers. Of course, it will only be a matter of time until law enforcement agencies change over. But this will be later rather than sooner since the cost involved in such a switch would be staggering.

While all CB transceivers are basically the same in circuitry, there are certain extra devices the more expensive models offer that can be important in highway use. For example, a mobile transceiver should be equipped with a "noise blanker." This will decrease or totally erase engine noises that can obstruct reception. On many less expensive models, this device is not built-in and it becomes necessary to purchase a noise suppression kit for the engine. This problem is not as prevalent in American cars as it is in foreign imports.

UHF/VHF Scanning Monitor Receivers

To reverse the tables on the police and listen in on their transmissions, UHF/VHF scanners are available. Crystal controlled to exact frequencies, these devices permit drivers to hear the actual radio communications between the police units and their chase cars and both to base.

What Is a Scanner?

A scanner is an electronic eavesdropping multichannel receiver that homes in on pretuned channels. It seeks out and locks in on each active channel, and then resumes scanning when the respective transmission is completed. It allows you to do to the police what their radar signals do to your car—seek and record.

How Much Does a Scanner Cost?

The retail price range is $129-229 for the popular crystal receivers. Many units require no crystals and employ programmed computer cards that allow vast scanning. These units can cost as much as $370.

How Do They Work?

Let's say that every day you must drive to work and home over a route that involves three police jurisdictions—state, county, and local. I do.

While there are reports available that give (for a price)

police radio frequencies across the United States, this information is also available free of charge from the Federal Communications Commission, Washington, D.C.

On my way to the office each day, I am subjected to radar traps set up by the Maryland State Police across Interstate 495, Montgomery County Police radar traps on county roads, and D.C. Metropolitan Police Department radar traps on certain wide, fast, straightaways like 16th Street.

My first step was to call the respective police departments and ask for their radio frequencies. This request was denied in all cases. So, I requested that the FCC provide me with the information. They did without hesitation or question. As an American citizen and taxpayer, I am part-owner of the air waves criss-crossing this land, air waves that the FCC administers and regulates for me! So are you. Drop them a line or walk in at 2025 M Street, NW in Washington, D.C. They'll even let you thumb through the books.

With the frequency information, I bought the corresponding crystals. These may be available at your local electronics store, or surely via mail from Radio Shack and/or Lafayette.

I inserted these crystals plus that one which corresponds to the U.S. Park Police (I short-cut through Rock Creek Park sometimes) into my scanner and I overhear not only their radar traps but everything else they are involved in.

Scanner and kindred monitors may be illegal in your state. Be sure to check this out prior to making a purchase.

CB is here to stay! While it may frustrate traffic cops, it has become a fact of life and there is very little they will be able to do about it. The federal government is even encouraging Citizens Band radio operators to organize a nationwide network.

Sponsors of the program think CB-ers may want to find out where "smokey" is in case of an emergency rather than to avoid him. Financed by the Department of Transportation, the same Federal Agency that demands state police forces enforce the 55-mph limit and prove it, this endorsement is confusing many law enforcement agencies. Caught in the middle, they are disunited and scattered in their opinion of CB. It may be good for highway safety but it's bad for their egos and bad for their quota systems. We have not seen the last legal battle between CB-ers and police.

CHAPTER 5

After You Get a Ticket

Bob Adams glanced up at his rear view mirror and felt his stomach twitch. The revolving red and white lights of a police cruiser were bouncing in the reflection.

He saw the police signal him over and he glanced down at the speedometer. The needle was to the right of 60. Bob tapped the brakes and began edging over toward the side of the road. He stopped his car and turned off the key. He glanced up at the mirror again. The cop car was also stopped about 20 yards behind him.

Bob took a deep breath and tried to think of what he was going to do. He was waiting for the cop to come up when he noticed he was signaling him to get out of his car and walk back to the police cruiser.

"Lazy bastard," Bob muttered. "They don't even get up to nail you anymore."

Bob climbed out and proceeded back to the black and white parked behind him.

"Is there something the matter? he said trying to sound cheerful and unconcerned.

"May I see your registration and driver's license," the officer said putting down his microphone.

"Certainly. Did I do something wrong?"

The officer said nothing, took the credentials and quietly examined them.

"You were exceeding the 55 mile-an-hour speed limit."

"Gee, was I? I mean I don't think I was. I've been driving for years and I've never been arrested for speeding. I always watch it to make sure I'm not going over the limit."

The cop's face was impassive. He began writing out the ticket.

"Officer, can't you give me a break? I've never had a ticket. I hate to ruin my perfect record."

The cop continued to write.

"Do you know Jim Wright?"

"No, sir."

"I went to school with him. He's on the Sheriff's patrol. You know any of those guys?"

The cop didn't answer. He grunted and continued to write.

"He'll tell you I'm a good guy. I support the police. I always donate to the police athletic fund . . . How about it? How about giving me a break?"

"Sorry, sir, I have my job to do."

"Maybe you're mistaken. Maybe you got me mixed up with someone else. Honest, I never speed."

"You were clocked doing 65 miles-per-hour on radar."

"On radar?"

"Yes, sir."

"The radar said I was doing 65?"

"Yes, sir. Sign here please."

"What's this?"

"It's a summons, sir. You can appear in court on the date indicated or you can enter a guilty plea by mail and send in the appropriate fine as indicated on the reverse side of the ticket."

"What if I don't sign it?"

"It doesn't matter, sir. You will still have to appear in court. The judge may or may not consider your willingness to cooperate."

"Can't you give me a break?"

"No, sir."

"You don't have a chance with this radar now."

"That's right, sir. There's no way to beat it."

"You mean I'm already convicted. I might as well go ahead and pay the fine?"

"Well, that's up to you sir. But if it was me and I got a ticket by radar I wouldn't bother wasting my time. Do you think the judge is going to believe you or the radar? But you're free to do what you want sir. You can fight it all the way to the Supreme Court but it won't change the fact that we got you on the radar and it has been my experience that when you're clocked by radar, you may as well pay the fine and get it over with, but like I said, it's up to you what you want to do. I'm not trying to influence you. But you asked me about radar and the radar never fails."

Bob looked glumly at the ticket then said: "There's no way you can take this back?"

"No, sir. Not with radar."

"Christ . . . nobody has a chance any more."

"Drive carefully, sir . . . and have a nice day."

When Bob got home, he complained loudly to his wife about the ticket.

"What are you going to do about it?"

"Pay it. What else?"

Bob Adams' experience is typical. Most Americans stand in awe of technology. We're led to believe that machines can do anything. There are computers which can solve mathematical problems in seconds which would take a man a year with pencil and paper. We've got electronics, and television and self-cleaning ovens. How do they work? Who knows? All we know is that they work.

In some ways we're no better off than primitive tribes in the jungles of Brazil who think a mirror is magic. When a cop tells us he has clocked us on radar and there's no beating it, many of us react just as Bob Adams did. Police radar is infallible. It's magic: there's nothing we can do about it when trapped by the latest technology.

But there's one flaw in that argument. The primitive in Brazil thinks a mirror is magic until he gets used to it and is no longer in awe of it. After a period of time he'll scrape off the back and recognize that he has a piece of glass with special stuff on it. Depending on how much education he gets, the primitive can end up knowing a lot about many things found in civilization. For instance, the Eskimos now whiz across the tundra on skidoos and hunt reindeer using rifles with telescopic scopes.

What do Brazilian natives and Eskimos have to do with police radar? Just this. There's nothing at all magical about radar. It's a man-made device and it's subject to man-made errors. It's a man-operated device and subject to man-caused errors.

Let's look at the way another driver handled a situation similar to the one in which Bob Adams found himself.

Jack Cramer is a salesman and he's on the road five days a week. Jack makes money talking to customers, not driving a car and so he figures that the less time he spends driving the more time he can spend selling and the more time he spends selling the more deposits he can make in his friendly neighborhood bank.

Jack speeds every day. He knows the law but he figures getting tickets is part of the risk of his business.

"If you're honest with yourself," Jack says, "you'll

admit that you also break the law every time you drive. If you doubt it, try actually driving 15 miles an hour—and no more—while passing through a school zone, and see how long it takes you to creep through. Or when you see the limit posted at 30 or 40 mph, actually drop down to that speed and maintain it and watch every car on the road flash by you and the guy behind you curse you.

"Most people just don't know how fast they are going most of the time. They slow down for the school zone but if they checked their speedometer they'd see they were way over the limit.

"I admit it. I break the law sometimes, but so do you. The big question is: 'Do you admit it?' But I want to make one thing clear. I'm not a reckless driver. I don't have accidents. Driving is part of my business and I'm serious about it. I'm careful and I don't take risks but I know my Caddie and I know the roads I travel and I use both safely and at the speed they were meant to be used at.

"Now I've had my share of tickets and I've paid most of them. But when they introduced the point system in my state and later when the federal government set the 55 mile-an-hour limit, I felt I was caught between a rock and a hard place.

"The fact that I'm on the road every day hustling between customers greatly increases my chance of getting a ticket. I had to decide whether I would lose money by making fewer calls or take my chances."

Jack discovered that it didn't take long for him to get two speeding tickets. In his state that added up to 6 points. If he got a total of eight points—any moving violation would give him an additional three—he would lose his license. Jack knew that if he lost his license he lost his livelihood. So he had to learn how to beat police radar.

Jack was tooling down the interstate at his usual clip when he saw the radar trap. The police car was parked below the crest of a hill; by the time Jack saw it he knew he'd been clocked. A half mile down the road the bubble gum lights were blinking and the cop in a cowboy hat was flagging him down.

Jack pulled over and stopped. He took a deep breath to relax and gain his composure then he reached into his glove compartment and pulled out a small notebook and a pen he had placed there for just such an emergency.

He saw a police officer writing out a ticket for one man and a second offender waiting behind him for his turn. Jack decided to sit tight for awhile. He lit up a cigarette and watched as one of the patrolmen came walking toward him. When the cop was next to him he hit the electric window button and before the lawman had a chance to speak, Jack said in a loud clear voice, "I'd like to have your name and shield number."

The cop was startled. For a second he remained speechless then he blurted: "You'll have to go down and talk to the corporal," and he pointed to his partner writing out the tickets.

"I'd like to see your identification first," said Jack.

"What? You some kind of wise guy? I said get out and go talk to the corporal."

"May I have your name and badge number?"

"No. Get movin'. We'll ask the questions."

Jack got out of the car and walked over to the other officer.

"I'd like to have your name and badge number and see some identification," he said firmly to the second cop.

"My name is Corporal Cooper. Shield number 76341."

Jack had him repeat it as he carefully wrote it down in his notebook.

"May I have your first name?"

"Thomas J."

"And may I see your identification?"

The corporal produced his police identification. While he was examining it he looked at the corporal and said, "The other man refuses to identify himself and he refuses to give me his name. I would like to know his name and see his identification."

"His name is Murezik."

Jack asked for the spelling and the first name and badge number. The officer was getting impatient but Jack had learned long ago that it's a waste of time to try the "Mr. Nice Guy" routine when you're nailed in a radar speed trap.

He was hoping the second cop would refuse to identify himself as is required. The corporal knew better and complied.

When the police officer took Jack's license and registration and climbed into the squad car to make the routine stolen car radio check, Jack made an elaborate display of walking to the front of the car and taking down the license number. Then he walked around to the side and took down the other identifying numbers on the vehicle.

The cop wrote out the ticket and handed it to Jack. "You were clocked doing 65 and the speed limit is 55."

"How was my speed determined?"

"By radar."

"I would like to inspect the radar reading."

"You can't."

"Is the radar reading the evidence you intend to use against me?"

"The judge decides that, we just give out the tickets."

"I believe the law says I'm entitled to see the radar

reading if you intend to use it in evidence."

"Well, the radar is a half a mile back up the road. You were clocked when you passed it and they radioed ahead and told us to stop your car."

Jack saw the cop on the road flagging down other cars and he knew that the trap car was not holding the setting but was busy clocking other cars.

"I'd still like to see the reading on the equipment."

"Well, you can't do that."

"Excuse me, corporal, are you formally refusing to allow me to inspect the radar reading which you are using as the basis of issuing a summons?"

"I'm not refusing nothing. The radar's not here, it's back up the road. Now if you will please sign this ticket, we have a lot of work to do here today."

"Certainly. I'll be happy to sign. Would you please give me the name and number of the officer who made the reading?"

"I don't know his name. You have to check with the officer on duty at headquarters for additional information, sir."

Jack signed the ticket, accepted his copy, and returned to his car. He knew the situation was a testy one and he felt he had pushed it as far as he could. The trick is not to get the cops so mad that they detain you. Jack struck just the right note of professionalism. He was firm, a man who knew his rights and was demanding them but at the same time making sure he was always polite and did not give the officers an excuse to overreact. The impression he wanted to create was that he knew exactly what he was doing and give the cops some pause about how they were performing their duties.

When Jack got back in his car he dictated a letter into his tape recorder which he would send to his secretary to type up. He told her to contact the police in this county and find out the name of the top man and send the following letter:

"On the advice of my legal counsel and in connection with a pending appearance on. . . ."

He read off the date and time and the name of the court he was to appear in. . . .

"I request the manufacturer's name, number, and model and any other identifying symbols for the particular piece of radiopositioning equipment in use on. . . ."

He gave the date and the approximate location. "I also need to know as an integral aspect of my defense your department's FCC license number, the date it was issued, and the expiration date of said license. Thank you for your kind cooperation and sign my name."

He also told his secretary to send it certified mail, with a return receipt requested. This is cheaper than registered mail yet provides the same evidence of receipt of the letter.

Jack knew the routine well. In his less affluent days, he typed up similar letters with two fingers. The idea was to make them sound legalistic and formal—and official.

Jack was on his way with his speedometer pushing once again above 55 but he had already laid down some important groundwork for his legal defense in court.

First off, he was creating evidence for his own defense. Usually a driver goes in and tells the judge his story while the cops come in with the papers. Judges like papers better than stories. Jack was on the way to getting a stack for the defense. He would have a copy of his letter asking for information for his defense and a receipt from the post office that the letter was delivered to the person it was addressed to. The odds with Jack were that when the sheriff or the head of a police barracks or chief or whomever receives such a letter, he will be confused about it. The confusion will cause delays. He'll check around to find out "What the hell is this all about?" He is even more likely to put it in a basket and forget it's there. Even if he honors your request, he's going to send it down through subordinates, and the request has a good chance to get bogged down in the bureaucracy.

Another thing Jack had going for him in his defense is the fact that the police officer refused to allow him to examine the radar reading and admitted that he had not observed the infraction himself but that the information had been passed on to him from the radar car.

Some lawyers argue that this constitutes hearsay evidence—that is evidence which is not testified to by a first-hand witness. The success of this ploy depends upon the skill of the attorney and the temperament of the judge. The point is that when Jack goes to court the case will not be cut and dried. He's muddied up the waters so that his attorney now has points to argue about.

A word about attorneys is in order. Jack always uses a lawyer. It is possible for a layman to go to court and beat a traffic ticket without a lawyer, but the odds are better with one. Not many judges or lawyers will admit it outside their closed circles, but they don't like to see nonlawyers defending themselves and winning—it's bad for business. When you've got a lawyer to talk to their lawyer, the legal eagles feel more comfortable. It's one thing for a citizen to come in and kick up a lot of fuss about his rights under the law and quite another when the fuss involves a payday for one of the brethern in the legal profession.

Another reason for hiring a lawyer is that he can keep an eye on the other side and make sure they don't pull a fast one. It can be expensive but how much is your driver's license worth to you?

Jack also makes it a practice to hire a local attorney when he has to appear in a strange city or county or state on a speeding violation. The same rule applies—judges feel more comfortable when they know one of their own is getting a payday out of the proceedings. Picking the right lawyer is a separate and distinct problem beyond the scope of this book, but suffice it to say find one you're comfortable with and one who is willing to fight the case and learn from your radar expertise.

Jack's motto is: "I can plead guilty without help. I need a lawyer to get me off."

Also a lawyer can save you valuable time. You may not have to appear at a hearing if your attorney is present and enters a plea of not guilty and requests a trial. Specifics such as these you have to work out with your attorney but in some states it's possible.

Jack Cramer's attitude is that there is no way he can function without his car. When he gets a ticket he considers it a threat against his economic life. As the cop writes the ticket Jack sees him as stealing the shoes off his kids.

"As far as I'm concerned, every ticket should be contested," Jack advises. "Most motorists operate on the theory that they will never get a ticket. I operate on the theory that I will and so I try to stack the deck in my favor as much as I possibly can. When I get a ticket I'm ready. Having a notebook and pen ready is an example of this.

"I've never met a person who does any amount of consistent driving—such as driving to work every day —who has not been nailed at least once. As far as I'm concerned, people who operate on the theory that they'll never get a ticket are playing it stupid.

"The second mistake the average driver makes is that when he gets his first ticket, he considers it a fluke and meekly pays the fine and collects the points. Most drivers don't wake up until they're on the ropes and are about to lose their license before they begin to fight back. Sad to say, by then it's often too late. They waited too long to fight.

"My advice: Fight the first ticket and every one you ever get. Never give the enemy any advantage. As far as I'm concerned, the cops are the enemy. They're trying to take away my license. They're trying to snatch the food from my baby's mouth. I give them nothing."

But even if you don't feel as strongly about the cops and speeding as Jack does, he still advises fighting your very first ticket. His reasoning is sound—and based on solid experience.

"When you receive your first ticket you are in your strongest position to fight," Jack says. "Your record is clean. The judge can be persuaded by a good story and a clean record. Once your license is stamped, once you've got a record of violations, then you're fighting at a distinct disadvantage.

"Look at it yourself. Say you were the judge. Who would you believe and let off? The guy with two speeding offenses fighting to prevent the loss of his license or the guy with the clean record who claims an injustice has been done to him?

"Once in a while I hear a story about a guy on the ropes and how the cops let him go or how the judge decides to give him a chance, but for me those are long odds. I say fight every ticket every time. There's nothing to say you won't lose fighting a citation but there is a chance you can win. If you lose fighting you're no worse off pointwise than if you throw in the towel.

"Another mistake many people make is that they think the cops always know what they are doing. Not so in my experience. Many cops, particularly those on small, poorly paid police forces, are often ignorant of the law. In recent years the courts have been very big on making sure defendants get their rights. The streets are full of muggers, crooks, rapists, and all sorts of weirdos let out there by bleeding heart judges.

"That's why it's important to take command at your very first meeting with the cop. Be the aggressor. Don't give him a chance to speak first. Ask him for his identification—he has to show you.

"Ask to see the radar equipment. They are obligated to show it to you. Be business-like. Get out your pad and start writing. Take down every number you can find. This throws the cops off. They wonder 'Who the hell I got here?'

"Most cops don't want to go to court. They often have to go during their free time. Most are afraid they will look like a fool on the witness stand when cross-examined by someone who is a real expert in radar or the law.

"You might even intimidate the guy out of giving you a ticket but don't count on it. The important thing to remember is that you act like you know what you are doing and don't become a wise guy or threaten the cops or mutter or act in any way that can be considered disrespectful. Treat them like confused children—firmly, but with compassion.

"If the officer lets you examine the radar unit, copy down all the identification information you can—the brand, model, serial number, anything you can find. Strange as it may seem, the police may be operating an illegal unit or one for which they are not properly licensed. When this is the situation your case will automatically be dismissed.

"If you have a passenger, have him or her join you. If you have several people in your car, have all of the adults come out and if you have enough notebooks give them all one and have everybody take notes.

"Whenever the cops say no or are evasive on any question, tell the others with you to note what has been said because they will be witnesses. For example say, 'Was this unit calibrated today?' When he answers tell your witnesses to note what he says. If he says "yes" ask if there is a record, because you will want to subpoena it. Ask several technical questions such as width of the beam, who determined what speed it would be set for, what is the Doppler error? Make notes of everything that's said. Ask the officer to repeat things. Say things such as, 'I want to be as fair to you as I can. Now would you please repeat that for me?'

"You'll have to use your own judgment on how far to go with this and how much you can get away with. Cops don't like to be made fools of, and so you must be on guard not to use a disrespectful tone."

Jack's theory is that you are creating evidence for your trial. Get as many officers involved as you can. The reason for this, he says, is that the more people who have to appear at a trial, the better the odds that some of them won't make it. When the complainants don't make it and the driver has a clean record, many judges will toss the whole thing out.

"Also, the more confusion you can create the better," says Jack. "For instance, if the cop doesn't know when the radar was last calibrated and admits it to you and you write that down or better still have a witness who hears it, he'll think twice before changing his story on the stand.

"Also when you write letters asking for information, as mentioned earlier, you add to the confusion. Write as many letters as you can, always using the phrase—"information is needed for my defense." You might ask for copies of the cop's training record concerning the operation of the particular equipment."

Jack will be the first to admit that these tactics can backfire and that you may have to appeal your case to win it. This costs money and it's a decision you'll have to make.

The central points of his argument are to fight every ticket, to go to court with as many pieces of paper as you can, and to create as many situations as you can which can be questioned and disputed in court. If you don't do anything until you get to court, you won't have ammunition to use in your fight.

CHAPTER 6

Beating the Odds

Jack Cramer and his attorney sat next to each other in the courtroom, anxiously waiting for the trial to begin.

When it did, events moved swiftly. The prosecution presented its case quickly. The defendant's car was clocked doing 65 miles-per-hour on a posted 55 mile-an-hour highway.

Officer Dundee testified that he was a qualified radar operator, noting that he had 12 years' experience operating various types of police radar.

Next came the cross-examination.

Defense attorney: "Officer Dundee, was this the only vehicle you clocked for radar violations on this date?"

Dundee: "No, sir. We clocked a great many."

Atty: How many?"

Dundee: "I can't say exactly, sir."

Atty: "Was it five or ten?"

Dundee: "It was more than that."

Atty: "Twenty or thirty?"

Dundee: "No, sir, more than that. We were set up for several hours."

Atty: "Did you clock more than 100 violators that day?"

Dundee: "Yes, sir. I'm not sure exactly how many, but I would definitely say there were more than 100."

Atty: "It was a good day for hunting?"

Dundee: "Yes."

The spectators and the jury all laughed.

"Tell me, Officer Dundee, do you specifically remember the defendant's car out of those hundreds?"

"No, sir. I don't."

"Yet you testify under oath that this particular driver was travelling at a precise speed?"

"Yes, sir."

"Tell the court how you can do this."

"Well, sir, the procedure is to clock the car and note the speed the radar records. Then we radio ahead to the advance cars and tell them the make, model, and color of the car and the speed it was travelling. They make note of it and we make a note of it on forms we have."

"After you call the information ahead what do you do next?"

"I clear the equipment and train in on another motor vehicle."

"In other words, as soon as you know the information is passed on to your partners down the road, you start hunting again?"

"That's right, sir."

Laughter filled the court again.

"What if the driver who allegedly breaks the speed limit wants to verify the radar reading?"

"He can't. He's down the road a half mile or a mile when he's pulled over."

"Are you aware that the alleged violator has that right? That he can request to see the radar reading?"

"Yes, sir. But as a practical matter no one ever does."

"Are you aware that the defendant asked to see the radar reading?"

"No, sir. He didn't ask me. I didn't talk to him at all. I received no such request all day."

"I see. If such a request had been made, could you have provided my client with the opportunity?"

"Yes, sir. Assuming that he made the request before I reset the equipment and that he was physically present to look at it."

"But since you received no request you immediately reset the equipment and put it back in service."

"Yes, sir."

"It was back in service before he was actually informed that he had violated the law—isn't that correct?"

"I'm not sure."

"Well he had to travel a considerable distance down the highway and after he was pulled over he had to wait for two motorists ahead of him to complete their transactions with your partners. That would take 15 minutes or more to occur. Did you wait that long before you put the radar back in service?"

"Well, sir, I can't testify specifically about this instance."

"At any time that day did you hold the radar out of service for 15 minutes or so, to allow the accused driver time to inspect the reading?"

"No, sir."

"All right. Now you testified earlier that you are an expert operator."

"Yes, sir. I've been operating for 12 years."

"Where did you learn this skill?"

"We are provided with in-service training by the department."

"What does this training consist of?"

"Well, we're shown how to operate the various types of equipment by other officers or in the case of new models, sometimes a factory representative checks us out."

"Do you learn how to repair the equipment?"

"No, sir. We just learn how to operate it."

"In other words, you are told which buttons to push and how to read the results but you are not really familiar with the technical operations of the equipment."

"We learn how to operate the equipment."

"Can you tell by looking at the equipment whether or not its working properly?"

"I can tell when I use it if it's on the blink but I can't tell by looking at it. If it jams up or something we report it and have it sent in for repairs."

"In other words, you know when it's broken but not necessarily whether or not it is working correctly when it's working."

"Well, I just know if it's working or not. If it's working, it's working right."

"How do you know that?"

"Know what?"

"How can you be sure the equipment is operating flawlessly? How do you know if the calibrations are correct? Did you personally calibrate the equipment on the day in question?"

"No, sir."

"Do you know how to calibrate?"

"Well I know how it works but I don't personally test it."

"So in other words you can't really testify as an expert that the equipment was working properly on the day in question."

"I have no reason to doubt it was working properly."

"Nevertheless you have no specific expertise which allows you to testify under oath that you know for an absolute fact, beyond any doubt, that the equipment was working flawlessly."

"As far as I'm concerned it was working fine."

"Do you have any testimony to offer which will prove to the court that you knew the equipment was working properly?"

"No. I'm certain it was okay, but I can't offer any proof that it was."

"Wouldn't it be more accurate to describe you as an operator rather than a radar expert?"

"Well I'm no expert on fixing them but I think I'm an expert in operating them."

"If we bring a radar engineer in here do you think you'll be able to answer his questions?"

"Yes."

"Would you be able to refute his testimony? Could you prove him wrong on certain technical points?"

"No, probably not."

"So much for this so-called expert witness your honor?"

Jack's attorney accomplished some important things in his questioning. He discredited the police officer as an expert witness. He downgraded him to an operator which means his testimony about the accuracy of the equipment is less valuable to the prosecution. The second point he established is that Jack was denied the opportunity to examine the radar reading because the equipment was already back in operation before Jack even made his request. A final point he established was that the radar operator had no specific knowledge or recollection of this particular case since he had clocked over a hundred cars that same day.

After the testimony, the attorney offered in evidence copies of letters Jack had written concerning the radar equipment and the signed receipt. He told the judge that these letters had been ignored by the police.

Next the attorney called Corporal Cooper to the stand.

Cooper testified that he remembered Jack well because he had asked so many questions and took notes. This was unusual enough for him to remember the incident.

"Officer Cooper, did you issue this ticket to the defendant?"

Cooper examined the ticket and said it was his signature and that he had issued it on the date. The attorney entered it into evidence.

"Officer Cooper, I note that you listed on this ticket in evidence that the defendant was driving his auto at 65 miles-per-hour. How did you determine that speed?"

"He was clocked on radar."

"Did you personally operate the radar?"

"No. As it was explained earlier, Officer Dundee operated the equipment and radioed the information ahead to us, telling us the make and model, color, and plate number of the car and the speed it was travelling. I noted this information on a form we use for this purpose."

"I don't want to belabor this, but just for the record, you issued the ticket strictly on the information supplied to you by Officer Dundee. You have no first-hand knowledge that the information given to you on the radio was exactly as it appeared on the radar."

"No, but Dundee is an experienced radar man and doesn't make mistakes."

"Indeed. I thought we were all prone to make errors from time to time but apparently Officer Dundee is the exception according to you. But never mind. Do you know how much time elapsed between the moment Dundee allegedly clocked the defendant and the time you notified him of the charge?"

"No, sir, I have no idea."

"Well, did you get to him the minute he pulled over to the side?"

"I don't remember. I was busy with other speeders. I just don't know how much time elapsed."

"I see. Are you convinced that your unit was following all police procedures exactly as prescribed that day?"

"Yes, sir."

"What is the procedure when a civilian asks a police officer for identification?"

"He is to identify himself verbally and show his credentials."

"Were you asked by the defendant for your identification?"

"Yes, sir."

"And did you produce it?"

"Yes, sir. I follow procedures exactly."

"And what about the other officers present. Were they following the proscribed procedures to the letter that day?"

"Yes, I believe they were."

"What about Officer Murezik? Was he following procedures to the letter?"

"Yes, sir, he was."

"That's strange. Didn't my client inform you that the man who turned out to be Officer Murezik had refused to properly identify himself when requested? Did you in fact supply my client with Murezik's name and inform Officer Murezik to supply his badge number?"

"I don't think Officer Murezik understood Mr. Cramer's request. When we understood what he wanted we supplied him with the information according to the regulations."

"Did my client ask for this information in some unusual way?"

"I don't know."

"When he asked you for the same information was it phrased in some way that made it difficult to understand?"

"I guess so."

"That's probably why you're a corporal and he's a patrolman?"

The spectators and the jury all laughed again.

"Tell me Corporal Cooper, do you remember when Mr. Cramer asked to see the radar reading?"

"Yes."

"What did you tell him?"

"I said the radar unit was a mile or so back down the road."

"Isn't it a fact that other cars continued to be flagged down and ticketed before the transaction involving you and Mr. Cramer was completed?"

"I don't remember."

"Did you attempt to call Officer Dundee and see if he had held the radar reading so it could be inspected?"

"No, I didn't."

"Why not?"

"Because the radar unit was down the road and there was no way to get back to it. We were on a divided highway and there was no way to turn around. He would have to walk back and I judged that it would be dangerous to allow a pedestrian to walk down the shoulder of the road for that distance."

"But you didn't give him that option? You didn't check with Dundee to find out if the reading had been preserved, did you?"

"No, sir."

"Do you suppose that as much as 15 minutes elapsed between the time Dundee allegedly clocked my client and the time he asked to inspect the reading?"

"I'm not sure. Could have been."

"Don't the procedures that you were following to the letter that day require you afford the defendant an opportunity to check the radar reading?"

"Yes. . . ."

"But you refused to do it? . . ."

"Well under the circumstances—yes. I didn't think it was safe to let him walk a mile or so down the highway."

"Isn't it a fact that you didn't bother to call Dundee to see if he had preserved the radar reading because you knew that he would have put the unit back in service after the amount of time which had elapsed."

"No, sir, I didn't know that."

"Well, I think everyone else in this room does."

Once again, the attorney undermined the credibility of the witness. He established that the police procedures were not followed in the routine request for identification and thus created a reasonable doubt that they were not followed in the radar arrest. Dundee had admitted that he put the unit back in service after recording the information and it now seemed reasonable that the motorist's right to inspect the radar reading had been abridged; that, in fact, the reading had long since been erased before the defendant even had a chance to request seeing it.

In his summation the attorney noted that the defendant's written requests for information concerning the radar had been ignored by the police, even though the letter clearly stated that it was needed for his defense. The lawyer noted that the records could be subpoenaed but this would mean rescheduling and more delays. He noted that the police procedures had been sloppy and that the proficiency of the machine had not been established. On the face of all of these things it seemed that there was a reasonable doubt about the whole proceeding being in order.

The judge agreed and ordered an acquittal.

CHAPTER 7

For You and Your Lawyer

If you decide to take an alleged speeding violation to court, do not forget that you are entering an arena which most motorists fear to enter. The average Joe or Jane will accept without contest whatever the policeman insists the violation was. The reasoning is that a fight in court is not worth the time and effort, and the cop must be right because he says so and he has the highly sophisticated electronic gear to back him up.

I hope that after reading this chapter, more and more citizens will fight for their rights and not capitulate. There are too many careful drivers who obtain speeding tickets and are convicted for offenses which they never committed.

Before starting, let me make a point; lawyers are not always necessary to win a favorable decision in a speed trap case. Some judges are sympathetic to a layman standing alone before the bench, defending himself. The defendant is merely the little guy, in the first place. *And,* the burden of proof is on the police. On top of this, equipped with the facts in this book, you will most likely know more about police radar, its ethical, legal, and technical uses, and its limitations as a highway speed monitoring device than the lawyers, police, and court together. However, if you were nabbed for reckless, drunken, or highly excessive speeds, forget it. You deserve what you get.

It's your personal decision whether or not to hire a lawyer. Don't make a snap decision. Give it some thought.

If you feel that the citation you have received was not warranted, it may be that the radar gear was not operating properly. Doppler error can occur at any time.

In Chapter 2 I discussed the properties of Doppler radar and, as you may recall, this standard emits a continuous wave signal. The big risk with this type of blanket signal is that almost any burst of energy (depending upon sensitivity) within the radar's field of coverage can cause a disturbance; a falling branch, flying bird, slammed car door, tossed rock, etc. I was told of a case in Wisconsin where it was proven that a barn nearby where a radar trap had been established had heavy machinery at work during the alleged violation. The police could not prove beyond a doubt that the radar beam was not affected by the loud noises and air disturbances in the area.

Sources of Doppler error can be divided into two categories; systematic (or bias) components and random (noise or accidental) components.

The table on page 87 will provide you with a synoptic overview of several possible causes.

For the less technical, other common causes of Doppler error are:

Ground Clutter. Strong permanent radar echoes returned by hills and buildings is often a limiting factor in a

TYPE OF ERROR	SYSTEMATIC COMPONENTS	NOISE COMPONENTS
Radar-dependent tracking errors	Discriminating zero setting and drift Gradient of receiver delay	Thermal noise Multipath Servo noise Variation in receiver delay
Radar-dependent translation errors	Transmitting oscillator frequency	VCO frequency measurement
Target-dependent tracking errors	Dynamic lag	Dynamic lag Target rotation
Propagation error	Gradient of atmosphere refraction	Fluctuation in atmospheric refraction

radar unit's performance, especially in mountainous terrain. Always make note of the terrain where the alleged infraction took place. Don't only look for hills and mountains, but observe if there are any thick stands of trees, mountains with loose rocks that might fall, and other such kindred objects between the roadway and the police radar beam.

Weather Clutter. The intervening atmosphere which must be traversed by the radio energy is homogeneous with respect to the refraction index at the radar's frequency. Always make note of the weather conditions at the time and place of the alleged infraction. In addition, see whether there are any electrical generators operating nearby or powerful radio transmitters, high power lines, and the like.

Rain and Snow. Both precipitations have a reflectivity factor. A fine example of this is the case cited in Chapter 1 involving Paul VanderMaat of Los Alamos, New Mexico. He was nabbed about 10 minutes before a thunderstorm, just as the oncoming electricity was creating ionized particles in the air that could easily throw radar out of kilter.

Sun. Uneven heating of the radar's components can cause Doppler error. Even a direct reflection of light can do it.

A good example of what such a reflection can do is best illustrated by the operating instructions provided by Tribar Industries, Ltd., Weston, Ontario, Canada, for its MUNI QUIP T3 Police Radar. Paragraph #8 states:

"Reduced range performance of the radar is usually caused by a deteriorated receiver schottky crystal (low sensitivity or high noise). Although the crystal is protected against damage due to direct reflection of the transmitted radar beam, it is not advisable to aim the unit against a metal surface such as the car floor or roof while in 'Radar Mode'."

Such facts can be devastating to the prosecution if they can be introduced and proven or at least used to show reasonable doubt. Remember the burden of proof is always on the police agency.

Ask to See the Unit

Your defense should really start on the shoulder of the highway. Always insist to the police officer that you be allowed to see the radar unit. Most will be accommodating. However, if your request is denied, this could be an important point in getting your case dismissed. So be sure to ask!

Make note of the make and model number of the radar unit. And don't be afraid to let the officer see you do it. Few people ever ask to see the radar unit, and those that do rarely take notes (because they wouldn't know what to do with them anyway). Your attitude may worry him a bit if he feels the least unconfident about his call. Most police try and stay out of court and thus avoid questions they cannot answer or on which they could exhibit their ignorance.

Get the officer's name, barracks, badge number, and the license plate number of his cruiser. This, together with a description of the speed trap set-up, weather conditions, locale, etc., will possibly be the most important step you'll take to win the case. Once you leave the scene, all this information is almost impossible to retrieve.

If the officer at the radar unit is not properly dressed this, too, can be a point in your favor. A friend in New England won a case several years ago because the state trooper operating the radar was technically out of uniform because his hat was off, he had no tie, and his sleeves were rolled up over his elbows. Going by the book, he was "off duty."

Was the Radar Properly Set Up and Checked Out?

Calibration. To fix, check, or adjust the gradations of measurement.

At the beginning of each work shift, the police officer is generally required to test the radar unit for accuracy via calibration. There are different types of calibration that may be used, depending upon the radar device. Here are several ways he may do it.

1. **Tuning Fork.** A small steel instrument with two prongs, when struck it sounds a certain fixed tone in perfect pitch. The tone will correspond with a set speed. Similar instruments are used for tuning musical instruments and ascertaining standard pitch.
2. **Automatic Calibration.** Many of the newer radar units have an automatic calibration device built in.

3. **Chase Car Calibration.** Some police will set their radar according to the reading registered by another police vehicle speeding through the beam. For example, the stationary vehicle will fire a radar beam across a particular stretch of roadway, and radio to the chase vehicle to drive into it at 55 mph. When this happens, the radar operator will adjust his unit accordingly.

There is a weakness in this type of calibration. Both testimonies become hearsay. Since the radar operator must take for a fact what the chase car driver says his speed is (he wasn't in the car to verify it) and, vice versa, the chase car driver must assume the radar operator locked in on 55 mph (he wasn't in the stationary vehicle to verify it), both men can only offer hearsay evidence. Then on top of this, a machine which has flaws (the chase car's speedometer) is being used to calibrate another machine which has flaws (or the radar would never have to be calibrated).

A good example of this point can be found in *People v. Offerman,* Supreme Court, Erie County, State of New York. The court held that evidence which included readings from radar device used to measure speed of automobiles, was not sufficient to sustain conviction. *Automobiles 353*

There are some other aspects entered on the case's record that you may find interesting and useful in defense.

1. Where, in prosecution for driving automobile at speed greater than that permitted by city ordinances, people relied entirely upon reading of dial on radar set, people had burden of establishing accuracy of such readings. Laws 1909, c. 570, 76, as amended.

2. In prosecution for driving automobile at speed greater than that permitted by city ordinances, where

radar device had been used to determine speed of automobile, testimony of police officer, who was driving police automobile used in testing radar device, that automobile speedometer agreed with reading of device as related to him over radio by operator of device and testimony of operator that device read same as speedometer reading relayed to him by other police officer were hearsay and improperly received in evidence. *Criminal Law 419 (1)*

3. In prosecution for driving automobile at speed greater than that permitted by city ordinances, wherein readings of radar device were relied upon to establish speed of defendant's automobile, failure of trial court to grant adjournment for the purpose of allowing production of an expert who could have testified concerning accuracy of radar device constituted an abuse of discretion. *Criminal Law 649 (2)*

(In number 3, above, you can see where the lower court denied the time to produce expert witness testimony. You have the right to request such witness testimony also if you feel the police are not sufficiently well versed in radar to operate it properly. Number 4, below, will show how this could be true!)

4. Acting chief of radio division of police department, who had been concerned with radio since 1910, but who had no experience with radar except for installation of radar device in police automobile under direction of his superior, and who had no formal training in radio, engineering or electronics, was not qualified to give opinion concerning accuracy of radar device, reading of which was used by prosecution to attempt to establish speed automobile had been driven in prosecution for driving at speeds in excess of that permitted by city ordinances. *Criminal Law 478 (1)*

5. Law enforcement should keep in stride with advances of science but science must not bring push-button justice unless and except such justice is surrounded by the long-established rules of evidence. *Criminal Law 650*

This entire case is available to you, cite as 125 N.Y.S. 2d 179. It is a perfect example of how hearsay evidence can be used and proof that all police are not expert with radar. Here we find an "expert" witness with no radar experience, except to install the instruments in the police cars under the supervision of a superior.

The Foundation for Your Case

It is a good rule to start by getting a complete rundown on the particular radar unit that was used to trap you. In Chapter 8 I provide a list of all the recognized and approved radar units, their trade names, frequencies, and manufacturers. While most manufacturers do not give out technical information on their units to the public (after all, the police forces, their bread and butter, might see this as a bit Machiavellian), this data is available from the Federal Communications Commission. Several of the files are not open and will have to be broken free under the Freedom of Information Act (FOIA). This is an easy procedure which is fully explained in Chapter 8.

The FCC files contain photographs of the actual equipment, electronic data, operating instructions (the do's and don'ts), frequency stabilities, emission limitations, calibrating procedures, and other esoteric information that may be of use in building a defense. You'll find it well worth the effort.

The *American Law Review* (ALR Digests, Evidence 537, 552) states that there are apparently no American decisions directly holding that evidence of measurements by mechanical or scientific instruments will be presumed correct in the absence of any evidence that the instrument has been properly tested for accuracy within a reasonable period. The respective FCC product information files will tell you how, when, and how often (in most cases) the equipment must be tested.

One of the most recent suits seeking to halt radar was filed in the United States District Court for the Eastern District of Oklahoma by Woody Bussey, also known as Wildhair, Indian Medicine Man, on behalf of himself and his young son, Scott Habib Bussey, against Secretary of Transportation Brock Adams.

The suit was filed on February 18, 1977, and at the time of writing no decision has been rendered. Nevertheless, it bears mention and watching. Copies of the actual complaint can be obtained via the Clerk, United States District Court, Eastern District of Oklahoma, Muskogee, Oklahoma 74402. What follows is the complete text of the complaint verbatim from the public record.

I cannot recommend using the logic Mr. Bussey adopts since its efficacy has yet to be proven.

Wildhair, Indian Medicine Man
a/k/a Woody Bussey, individually
and for his minor child:
Scott Habib Bussey and similarly
affected citizens
Plaintiffs
vs.
Brock Adams
Secretary of Transportation
Defendant

77 - 47 - C
FILED
Feb. 18, 1977

COMPLAINT

Comes now the plaintiffs and invokes the jurisdiction of the court to hear the proceedings outlined below, based on: The Federal Tort Claims Act, 28 U.S.C.A. § 2671-2680, 1346 (b), 1402 (b), 1504 (b), 2110, 2401, 2402, 2411, 2412, and 1356, passed by the Congress to provide redress to individuals aggrieved by torts committed or permitted by the United States plus the 8th Amendment to the Constitution.

1.

Plaintiffs bring this action for an interlocutory injunction under USCA 2282 and 2284, to restrain the Secretary of Transportation, Brock Adams, from permitting the use of radar emissions on or along any road, highway, or street financed in any way with federal funds. For the reason that said usage of radar emissions are dangerous and violate the constitutional rights of plaintiffs under the Eighth Amendment to the Constitution.

2.

Plaintiffs are citizens of the United States of America and citizens of the State of Oklahoma wherein they reside.

3.

Defendant, Brock Adams, is Secretary of Transportation of the United States of America, duly appointed and approved by the proper authorities and is serving in that capacity at this time. Defendant Brock Adams is not a resident of the State of Oklahoma but rather is a resident of the District of Columbia.

4

The amount in controversy exceeds ten thousand dollars and there is diversity of citizenship between the parties.

5.

To permit law enforcement officers to haphazardly broadcast radar emissions along highways, roads, or streets that are financed in whole or part by federal funds, is using a wartime weapon, radar, to endanger the health and lives of United States citizens and is contrary to the Eighth Amendment of the Constitution which prohibits cruel and unusual punishment.

6.

Our State Department complains that the Russians have used microwaves, radar, to harass United States employees in a harmful manner. This is done daily to citizens of the United States to try and enforce the fifty-five mile speed limit.

7.

The fact that of the *hordes* driving vehicles on highways and streets where this harmful weapon, radar, is used, *relatively few* are arrested for excessive speeding. *To paraphrase Mo Tzu, the Chinese sage of antiquity: "A system that cures four or five persons out of ten thousand of the speeding habit cannot be called a practical solution."* (Emphasis added.)

8.

Radar emissions are not selective in seeking out law-breakers but rather bathe all citizens within their range with the same harmful microwave emissions. This is true of non-speeders in vehicles as well as the non-drivers and non-riders of vehicles who happen to be in the path of these beams.

9.

Radar emissions are used to cook foods in microwave ovens as is shown on television, wherein one commercial shows an athlete racing down the clock to see whether he can arrive home before a radar range can *defrost* then cook a roast completely. To date, the radar range has won.

10.

Plaintiffs contend that the same radar emissions or microwaves that are efficient in the kitchen are to a degree, as efficient in the interior of a vehicle as well as within the human body. *The human fetus too is not immune to the potential harm done to human tissues.*

11.

Plaintiffs contend that the cauterizing effect of radar emissions are harmful and in effect, cause cardiac arrest, damage to the optic nerves and create actuate epilepsy conditions. *Perhaps this may be the cause of so many one-car accidents.*

12.

One truck driver complained to plaintiffs that when his Fuzzbuster showed that he was within radar emissions, his eyeballs became so irritated that they seemed on the point of bursting. He suffered from glaucoma yet was not uncomfortable until his Fuzzbuster was activated.

13.

The program *60 Minutes,* shown on national television on February 13, 1977, told of the difficulty the Navy was having in trying to locate the Seafarer's Sanguine Project antennae within the United States. Some scientist on the program said that even these low voltage antennae were so dangerous that he wouldn't let his family live near its location and plaintiffs contend that radar emissions are more dangerous.

14.

Plaintiff Woody Bussey asks the court to take Judicial Notice of the potential damage that may be caused to citizens by the use of radar emissions and the fact that he fears for the safety of his minor child, that this minor and others are subject to potential genetic damage and are due the protection of the court.

15.

Plaintiffs sue on their own behalf and on behalf of other American citizens similarly affected, pursuant to Rule 23 of the Federal Rules of Procedure. The class consists of several hundred million citizens. This class is so numerous that joinder of all members is impracticable; there are questions of law and fact common to the class; the claims of the representative plaintiffs are typical of the claims of the class; the representative plaintiffs will fairly and adequately protect the interests of the class; the defendant has acted on grounds generally applicable to the class; the prosecution of separate actions by individual members of the class would create a risk of inconsistent or varying adjudications or adjudications with respect to individual members of the class which would as a practical matter be dispositive of the interests of other members not parties to the adjudications or substantially impair or impede their ability to protect their interests; and questions of law and fact common to members of the class predominate over any question affecting only individual members, so that as a class action is superior to other available methods for the fair and efficient adjudication of the controversy.

Wherefore plaintiffs respectively pray for an interlocutory injunction against the defendant named herein, enjoining him from further permitting the use of radar emissions on any highways or streets paid for in part or whole by federal funds and that said Eighth Amendment to the Constitution be upheld and the cruel and unusual punishment of citizens by radar emissions be stopped immediately, and that upon proper hearing, said defendant be permanently enjoined from further permitting the use of radar emissions against human beings.

Attack the Police Expertise

It is essential for a radar operator to possess enough knowledge and ability to understand when the radar equipment he is operating is unsatisfactory, giving inferior performance or unsound data. This knowledge and ability can be obtained *only* by a complete and suitable training program; experience by itself or incomplete training can be detrimental and lead to misinterpretation of the radar picture.

Did you know that some units take 30 minutes to warm up?

Some handheld antennae cannot be rotated or panned.

Most units demand proper collimation (line of sight adjustment).

Certain units can lock in on a fast-moving object within a group of moving objects; however, the police officer must be able to determine which vehicle is violating the posted speeds. Many officers become confused in such "hunting" situations.

Speed

The speed of your vehicle is a matter of opinion, either by an expert or a non-expert witness. Below are some cases you may wish to research while building a defense.

1. The observed data as to a moving vehicle cannot sufficiently be set out before a jury, therefore you or a witness may state an opinion as to the speed. *See:* Ellison v. Evans, 85 Ga. App. 292, 69 S.E. 2d 94 (1952); 32 C.J.S.

Evidence 546 (51 thru 54); Ga. Digest, West Pub. Co., Evidence, Key Nos. 471 (23), 474 (8), 492.

2. If you or your witness have an opinion as to speed based on observation, you may state that observation even though you made no estimate as to the speed and formed no opinion at the time of observation. *See:* Engle v. Finch, 37 Ga. App. 389, 140 S.E. 632 (1927).

3. The witness need not have seen the vehicle but may base his opinion on seeing the headlights and hearing the noise of the motor. *See:* Hill v. Kirk, 78 Ga. App. 310, 50 S.E. 2d 785 (1948), or on the sound of the motor alone. *See:* Murphy v. Atlanta, 64 Ga. App. 752, 14 S.E. 2d 232 (1941).

Each state will have its own cases on which you will be able to draw. Your local library will undoubtedly have law digests which can provide the specific information you'll need. A good place to start is the rules and regulations concerning the testing of speedometers and speed meters.

WAS THE RADAR UNIT LEGAL?

There are two areas in which the police can slip up: (1) they may be operating unlicensed radar equipment, and (2) the radar unit itself may never have been sent to the FCC for type acceptance.

Just like CB-ers, police departments *must* secure operating permits from the Federal Communications Commission before they are allowed to operate radiopositioning equipment. And, like CB licenses, their paper holds them to the use of only the amount of units listed on the license. Many police departments are smart: they will take out a license for more units than they need as a cover. Other police agencies will take out a license for a few units and then forget to up-date it when they expand. In this case, the unlicensed units are illegal. For the most current information on the number of units any police agency (local, county, campus, turnpike, park, state, etc.) has, write to the Federal Communications Commission, International Operations Division, 1919 M Street, NW, Washington, D.C.

In Chapter 8 I have provided a listing of licensed state police radiopositioning equipment for all 50 states, Guam, and Puerto Rico as of 1976. But this list can change almost daily. Use this list only as a guideline. This book alone may cause police agencies to check out their licensing.

If a police force is licensed for 10 radar units (output 5w—Frequency 10,525) and they are operating 20 units (output 5w—Frequency 10,525) the burden of proof as to which units are legal and which are not is not on you. The police must prove beyond a shadow of doubt that the unit used on you is legal. They will also have to show that the extra ten units have not been used against motorists pending approval of a license amendment.

How do you find out how many units the police are using? Ask them for the information. If they fail to provide it, ask the court to obtain it for you, based upon your suspicions. For example, the state police of California were only licensed for 5 units (5w output—Frequency 2455) as recently as early 1976. I think you could assume they may be using more than this!

Some states have Sunshine Acts that will break such information free.

It must always be remembered that a radiopositioning unit must be type-approved by the Federal Communications Commission before it can be offered for sale, sold/or used legally by police agencies. There are no laws that prevent an individual or a company from developing such devices but, before they can be offered commercially, the FCC's Technical Standards Branch must approve them.

One might think that the major manufacturers would be too well organized and sophisticated ever to allow themselves negative exposure in this clearly defined area of control. This was not the case on at least one occasion, according to an exchange of letters I found while researching this book.

The incident involves the president of a major radiopositioning manufacturing firm alerting the Federal Communications Commission that one of his competitors was soliciting and accepting orders on a traffic radar device without having already secured the necessary type-approval.

Washington shot a letter back to the manufacturer and asked if the charges were valid. The project engineer in charge of the particular product insisted that none had been sold and that they were using the equipment in a "marketing research effort." It was stopped immediately with a letter to field sales representatives.

In citing this case, I do not in any way want to suggest that this practice is widespread throughout the industry. Nevertheless, it proves that the driver accused of an alleged speeding violation may possibly find the gear used by the police agency on said occasion was not yet type-accepted. It also shows that information one may not be directly seeking could pop out of an FCC file search!

Put the Cop on the Stand

Your goal here is to attack the police officer's credibility. Ask the officer to take the stand for some direct or cross-examination (depending upon the circumstances). Always try and point out grey areas—areas of reasonable doubt.

DON'T COME ON LIKE PERRY MASON!
DON'T BE OVER-CONFIDENT!

Just where the line lies between a helpful and a harmful cross only experience can teach. If you elect to have counsel, make sure you retain one who is "at home in the courtroom." It wouldn't hurt if the lawyer knew the judge; not that judges are not fair-minded (eminently so!) in the conduct of trials, but they are human, and the trial lawyer who knows his judge will start with an advantage.

The following questions might help you to bring that critical amount of reasonable doubt into the case:

1. At the time of the alleged infraction, how long had it been since the radar unit was last calibrated? By which method? How often must this particular unit be calibrated? If not properly calibrated, what is the drift factor or error ratio?

2. At what frequency does the radar unit operate? What is its licensed output? When was it last tested for frequency tolerance? By whom? Was the unit's transmitter and antenna properly matched at the time of the alleged infraction? What is the degree of impedance?

3. What is the total extent of your training with such equipment? How many hours of schooling? Could you recognize a problem with it if something happened? Do you hold any FCC licenses? Does your Master Technician hold a First Class or Second Class Radio License?

4. Do you have *any* kind of quota? Must you stop so many vehicles per day? Per month? Per year? If so, how

many? If you do not meet a particular quota what happens to you? Remember you are under oath!

5. Why did you select that specific location for setting up the unit? What is given consideration in selecting said locale? Why? What is ground clutter? Weather clutter? Can the hot sun or reflections affect your unit's performance? Rain? Snow?

6. What was the width of the gun's beam at the point my car entered it? How far did the beam extend from the police cruiser? Did you visually sight my alleged violation? Beyond a doubt? Remember you are under oath!

7. Did you set the radar meter higher than the posted speed to compensate for error, drift, or to give motorists a grace space? If yes, who decided on the setting? On what basis? By whose authority?

The conduct of a case before the Bar is a peculiar art for which many lawyers, however learned in the law, are not fitted. Add to this the esoteric nature of a radar speeding violation, and you may be better off handling it yourself. Lawyers have a saying: "A lawyer who represents himself has a fool for a client." A layman who represents himself on such minor problems may impress the judge with his knowledge of the electronic equipment, its limitations, and ethical uses. The better one is at developing the facts, the better for the case. Most police agencies and courts are not accustomed to hearing lay people run off points of law and issues of fact, clearly defined and presented to the court in the least possible words. A wise man once said, "In confusion there is profit." Catch 'em off guard!

CHAPTER 8

The Information Bank

NATIONWIDE STATE POLICE FREQUENCIES FOR RADIOPOSITIONING EQUIPMENT (PLUS GUAM AND PUERTO RICO)

The list below was taken from the Federal Communications Commission's files in 1976. Licenses are constantly being updated and changed. *This is merely to be a guideline.*

REMEMBER:

a. When making your request be specific as to which law enforcement agency(ies) about which you want license information.

b. *Never* ask for radar licenses, *always* say radiopositioning.

c. If you live near an FCC Field Office (see list in this chapter) it may be a good place to start for information.

d. All licenses are issued by the FCC, Washington, D.C. No state or local agency can license radio equipment.

For current information on your state police or local police *radar* unit licenses just write: International Operations Division, Federal Communications Commission, 1919 M St., NW, Washington, D.C.

STATE	FREQUENCY	UNITS	OUTPUT
ALABAMA	10,525	300	5w
ALASKA	10,525	2	5w
ARIZONA	10,525	50	5w
	10,525	170	.2w
	2,455	10	3w
ARKANSAS	10,525	16	3w
	10,525	23	5w
CALIFORNIA	10,525	20	3w
	2,455	5	5w
COLORADO	10,525	75	3w
CONNECTICUT	10,515	15	3w
	10,525	20	5w
DELAWARE	10,525	4	3w
	10,525	15	5w
FLORIDA	2,455	5	3w
GEORGIA	10,525	150	3w
HAWAII	—	—	—
IDAHO	10,525	10	3w
	2,455	12	3w
ILLINOIS	10,525	300	5w
INDIANA	10,525	105	3w
IOWA	10,525	250	5w
KANSAS	10,525	225	3w
KENTUCKY	10,525	101	3w
LOUISIANA	10,525	60	5w
MAINE	10,525	65	3w
MARYLAND	10,525	50	3w
	10,525	100	5w
MASSACHUSETTS	10,525	75	3w
MICHIGAN	10,525	30	5w
MINNESOTA	10,525	179	3w

STATE	FREQUENCY	UNITS	OUTPUT
MISSISSIPPI	10,525	300	5w
MISSOURI	10,525	250	3w
MONTANA	2,455	20	3w
NEBRASKA	10,525	20	3w
NEVADA	10,525	50	3w
NEW HAMPSHIRE	10,525	50	5w
NEW JERSEY	10,525	28	3w
NEW MEXICO	10,525	45	3w
NEW YORK	10,525	58	3w
NORTH CAROLINA	10,525	400	5w
NORTH DAKOTA	10,525	*listed by individual cities*	
OHIO	10,525	40	3w
	10,525	340	5w
OKLAHOMA	10,525	250	5w
OREGON	10,525	70	3w
PENNSYLVANIA	10,525	150	5w
RHODE ISLAND	10,525	46	3w
	2,455	4	3w
SOUTH CAROLINA	10,525	110	3w
SOUTH DAKOTA	10,525	100	3w
TENNESSEE	10,525	1	3w
TEXAS	10,525	23	5w
UTAH	2,455	5	3w
	10,525	25	3w
VERMONT	2,455	6	3w
	10,525	13	5w
	10,525	13	3w
VIRGINIA	10,525	210	5w
WASHINGTON	10,525	110	3w
	2,455	20	3w
WEST VIRGINIA	10,525	115	3w
WISCONSIN	10,525	60	3w
WYOMING	10,525	41	5w
GUAM	10,525	4	3w
PUERTO RICO	10,525	1	180w

FCC-TYPE ACCEPTED RADIOPOSITIONING UNITS
MANUFACTURERS—TYPES—FREQUENCIES

The manufacturers listed below all produce FCC type-accepted radiopositioning equipment. The list is current at the time of writing and should not change greatly for some time. Police agencies do not change their radar very frequently due to the cost factors. The manufacturers will most likely add to their lines but still retain those units in use. This list should be a guideline. Updates and information on new units, etc., can be secured from the Federal Communications Commission by writing:

Laboratory Division
Federal Communications Commission
Chief Engineer
P.O. Box 40
Laurel, Maryland 20810
Telephone: (301) 953-9850

For your convenience, I have also given the addresses and telephone numbers of the radar manufacturers here and in Canada.

MANUFACTURER	TYPE	FREQUENCY RANGE
1. Kustom Electronics, Inc. 1010 West Chestnut St. Chanute, Kansas 66720 (316) 431-4380	MR-8 MR-7 TR-6	24050-24250 10500-10550 10500-10550
2. Decatur Electronics, Inc. 725 Bright Street Decatur, Ill. 62522 (217) 428-4315	715 DCP HAC RA-GUN	10500-10550 10550-10550 10550-10550 10550-10550
3. CMI, Inc. 408 Pine St., Drawer D Minturn, Col. 81645 (303) 476-3171	JF 100	10525-10525

MANUFACTURER	TYPE	FREQUENCY RANGE
4. Smith & Wesson Electronics Co. Meridian Road Eaton Town, N.J. 07724	1-022-2438-00 1A-002-2000-00	10525-10525 10525-10525
5. West Bend Autotronics, Inc. 684 Indiana Avenue P.O. Box 492 West Bend, Wis. 53095 (414) 334-3020	4000CP DHH6000 MVR5000	10500-10550 10500-10550 10500-10550
6. Sentry Research Corporation P.O. Box 2470 Texarkana, Ark. 75501 (501) 772-9911	SR-10 SR-4 MINI DUAL SR-8 SPEEDREADER	10500-10550 10500-10550 10500-10550
7. Champion Electronics, Inc. Suite 200D 9821 Katy Freeway Houston, Texas 77024	JF 100	10525-10525
8. Automatic Signal Division-LFE Corp. Regent Street East Norwalk, Ct. 06856 (203) 838-4791	RD-2 RD-R2 RD-R2F S-5	2454-2456 2454-2456 2454-2456 10510-10525
9. Tribar Industries, Ltd. 3650 Weston Rd., Unit 19, Weston, Ontario Canada M9LIW2 (416) 749-6000	4400-C MUNI QUIP T3	10525-10525 10500-10550
10. Westinghouse Air Brake Co. Union Switch & Signal Division of Swissvale Post Office Pittsburgh, Pa. 15218 (412) 823-3400	DR-30 DR-40	10525-10525 10525-10525
11. Boeing Aerospace Co. P.O. Box 24666 Seattle, Wash. 98124 (206) 773-2039	Pacer II Pacer III	10500-10550 10500-10550
12. General Signal Corp. 801 West Avenue Rochester, N.Y. 14611 (716) 436-6511	59366-1	10525-10525

REMEMBER:

1. If the unit used to trap you is not one of those listed here, take note of it because it may not be type-approved yet. And if it is not, the unit is totally illegal.

2. If you feel that road, traffic, weather, calibration, or other factors may be in your favor, call the manufacturer and discuss with him the esoteric limitations of his firm's equipment. If this fails, call or write the FCC. In both instances, get the responses in writing for use in the courtroom.

While many of the manufacturers I have spoken with were reluctant to send me sales flyers or brochures (much of this information I was then able to get via the FCC), the representatives of the companies did speak frankly with me about their products. A few said that they would honor my request for information if I sent it in on letterhead explaining the reason I wanted it.

The greatest problem the manufacturers find with the radar devices turns out to be the human beings operating them. One vice-president of a major manufacturing firm told me, with the agreement his name would be off the record, that those most interested in properly training a team to operate the units are state police forces. The real problems arise in small towns when anybody can just pick up a unit and go out on a fishing expedition. "Hell, some of the radio engineers on hick town forces can't even fix their own radios—so how does anyone expect them to understand the intricacies of radar?" he added.

I even met a sales representative for a radar manufacturer who has both a radar detector and CB radio in his car. Why? He told me that knowing what he knows about the people he sells his line to, you need the protection. "How can you expect a guy to understand these gadgets after reading a sales brochure and a list of operating instructions? And some of that gear really takes a beating," he continued. "It's not theirs, so they don't give a damn about how it is bounced around, left out in bad weather conditions, or stored."

THE FREEDOM OF INFORMATION ACT

The Freedom of Information Act (FOIA) was enacted in 1966 and greatly amended in 1974. The philosophy behind it is that all records in the possession of a federal agency should be available for public inspection.

Although the states are not bound by the Act, many states do have their own Freedom of Information Acts which are sometimes called "Government in the Sunshine Laws."

Since the frequencies are assigned by the Federal Communications Commission, and it too must type-accept all radar devices utilized by police agencies, the Agency's files fall into the scope of the FOIA.

When I requested several files once, there was no need to engage FOIA; the FCC personnel handed over exactly what I requested. Government agencies cannot just say files are not available, the FOIA rules and regulations are pretty strict. I've listed a synoptic overview of the seven exemptions the government may use to withhold documents from disclosure. Before you request anything, it will be better if you acquire a copy of the Act itself or an explanation of it. Sources are listed later in this chapter.

Title: Freedom of Information Act, 5 U.S.C. 552. This means that you will be able to find the Act in Volume 5 of the U.S. Code, section 552. The Code will be in the reference room of law libraries and most law offices.

Request: According to the law, you must "reasonably describe" the records you want. You do not need the formal name of the document. Just describe it well enough so that it can be found without much trouble. Give all the details you have. In the case of radar equipment type-acceptance files, give the manufacturer's name, address, the unit in question, and the frequency. Address the letter to the FCC's general counsel. Give your telephone number in the letter to make things move a bit quicker!

Cost: The law provides that the government can assess "reasonable standard charges for document search and duplication." It also states that these fees can be waived if the agency decides that the public at large might benefit from the release of the material. Your request may also set a limit on such charges.

Time Schedule: A request for information *must* be answered within 10 working days. If some or all of the information is refused, you must be told of your right to appeal and given the name of the official, usually the agency director, who will rule on it. With some exceptions, the decision must be made within 20 working days from the time the appeal is filed. If documents are denied, an appeal should be registered (with copies of your original request and the denial).

If you lose the appeal or there is no answer within the prescribed time, you may file suit in federal court.

Exemptions: There are seven justifications in the law for refusal to disclose information.

1. Secret documents: "in the interest of national defense or foreign policy." Under the 1974 amendments, however, federal courts may examine a claim of national security to see if it is being used to suppress data that could be politically embarrassing but not actually sensitive. Also, proper classification of a few pages of a document does not justify secrecy for the entire report.

2. Documents that do not affect the public and are "solely" related to the internal personnel rules and practices of an agency."

3. Documents maintained confidential by federal law, such as income tax returns, applications for patents, and completed census forms.

4. Trade secrets and commercial or financial data furnished by a person or company on a privilege or confidential basis.

5. Inter-agency or intra-agency communications, with views and recommendations of officials on policy or legal issues. This does not apply to reports or analyses.

6. Personnel and medical files.

7. Investigatory records put together for law enforcement (such as FBI files) but only if their disclosure would: (a) interfere with law enforcement; (b) deprive a person of a fair trial; (c) constitute an unwarranted invasion of privacy on a personal level; (d) unveil the identity of a confidential source; (e) disclose investigative techniques or sources; (f) endanger the life or physical safety of a law enforcement officer. For the exact wording it is best to check the U.S. Code before submitting each request you may have.

Here are a few pointers to make your FOIA request move faster.

1. Mail your request to the proper office the first time. If it reaches the wrong office they may forward it, and the time limit by which the agency must react to your demands will not begin until it reaches the proper office.

2. Watch the deadlines. Don't allow the agency personnel to get the feeling you are not anxious to receive the materials.

3. While the Act permits agencies to charge for photocopies of released information, many agencies do not charge if the costs are under a certain amount. Make sure you clearly understand this point. But remember that the agencies cannot charge you for the time their lawyers and officials spend in deciding whether or not to grant your request.

4. Keep copies of all correspondence with the agency.

5. Give your telephone number.

6. Appeal to the head of the agency from an initial adverse decision.

If you need additional assistance or information concerning the Act, you may want to contact one of the following organizations:

The Reporters Committee for Freedom of the Press
Room 1112
1750 Pennsylvania Avenue, N.W.
Washington, D.C. 20006
(202) 298-7460

Freedom of Information Clearing House
2000 P Street, N.W.
Washington, D.C. 20036
(202) 785-3407

Freedom of Information
School of Journalism
Box 858
University of Missouri
Columbia, Missouri 65201
(314) 882-4856

For detailed discussions of the Act, please refer to the following sources:

"The Freedom of Information Act: A Seven Year Assessment," Vol. 74, *Columbia Law Reporter*, beginning at page 895 (June, '74).

Attorney General's Memorandum of the 1974 Amendments to the Freedom of Information Act, published by the United States Department of Justice. Available for 90¢ from the Superintendent of Documents, U.S. Government Printing Office, Washington, D.C. 20402.

Freedom of Information Act and Amendments of 1974—Source Book: Legislative History, Text and Other Documents, published by the Committee on Government Operations, U.S. House of Representatives, and the Committee on the Judiciary, U.S. Senate. Available for $4.80—Stock No. 052-070-02805-0, U.S. Government Printing Office, Washington, D.C. 20402.

SAMPLE LETTER REQUEST (FOIA)

General Counsel
Federal Communications Commission
Washington, D.C.

Sir:

Pursuant to the Freedom of Information Act, 5 U.S.C. 552, I hereby request access to, or a copy of, (describe the document) together with all appendices, annexes, or other materials attached to the (document).

If any expenses in excess of $_____ are incurred in connection with this request, please inform me in advance for my approval. (You may ask that fees be waived if you feel the information could be considered as "primarily benefiting the public.")

If you determine that some portions of the (document) are exempt from the release, I request that you provide me with the remainder. I reserve my right to appeal any such decisions.

If you do not grant this request within 10 working days, I will consider my request denied.

Sincerely,

FCC

Field Offices: Address all communications to the Engineer-in-Charge. Exact street addresses may be found in local telephone directories under "United States Government."

Alabama, Mobile 36602
Alaska, Anchorage (Box 644) 99501
California, Los Angeles 90014
California, San Francisco 94126
California, San Pedro 90731
Colorado, Denver 80202
D.C., Washington 20555
Florida, Miami (Box 150) 33101
Florida, Tampa 33606
Georgia, Atlanta 30303
Georgia, Savannah (Box 77) 31402
Hawaii, Honolulu 96808
Illinois, Chicago 60604
Louisiana, New Orleans 70130
Maryland, Baltimore 21202
Massachusettes, Boston 02109
Michigan, Detroit 48226
Minnesota, St. Paul 55102
Missouri, Kansas City 64106
New York, Buffalo 14203
New York, New York 10014
Oregon, Portland 97205
Pennsylvania, Philadelphia 19106
Puerto Rico, San Juan (Box 2987) 00903
Texas, Beaumont (Box 1527) 77704
Texas, Dallas 75202
Texas, Houston 77002
Virginia, Norfolk 23510
Washington, Seattle 98104

I hope that after reading this book you will never sit back again and accept another alleged speeding violation without giving them a fight (unless, of course, you are caught trying to break a land speed record on a public roadway!). There are too many stories about mass ticketing campaigns and the so-called interstate goon squads confiscating radar detectors as harassment.

Ask questions! Insist upon being witness to an immediate, roadside calibration. Make notes—openly. And always bring a witness along when one is available.

Everything has limitations just like radar itself. CBs are only as good as the people providing the information over the airwaves about upcoming traps, the detectors may pick up airport vector signals as well as radar emissions, and all the legal defenses are subject to human interpretation. It is simply my sincere wish that every driver on America's roads today be equipped to fend for himself against the all-too-frequent entrapment procedures, faulty electronic gear, and harassment activities engaged in by many police agencies. Safe driving!

Index